EVOLUTIONARY INTUITIONISM

Evolutionary Intuitionism

A Theory of the Origin and Nature of Moral Facts

BRIAN ZAMULINSKI

McGill-Queen's University Press
Montreal & Kingston • London • Ithaca

ISBN 978-0-7735-3111-6 (cloth)
ISBN 978-0-7735-3158-1 (paper)

Legal deposit first quarter 2007
Bibliothèque nationale du Québec

Printed in Canada on acid-free paper that is 100% ancient forest free (100% post-consumer recycled), processed chlorine free.

This book has been published with the help of grants from the Academic Participation/Professional Development Fund and the Publications Fund of the University of Saskatchewan.

McGill-Queen's University Press acknowledges the support of the Canada Council for the Arts for our publishing program. We also acknowledge the financial support of the Government of Canada through the Book Publishing Industry Development Program (BPIDP) for our publishing activities.

Library and Archives Canada Cataloguing in Publication

Zamulinski, Brian Edward, 1951–
Evolutionary intuitionism: a theory of the origin and nature of moral facts / Brian Zamulinski.

Includes bibliographical references and index.
ISBN 978-0-7735-3111-6 (bnd)
ISBN 978-0-7735-3158-1 (pbk)

1. Ethics, Evolutionary. I. Title.

BJ1311.Z34 2006 171'.7 C2006-905201-8

This book was typeset by Interscript in 10.5/13 Sabon.

For my cousin Naomi,
and in memory of
my mother, Mary,
and my aunt Eileen

Contents

Acknowledgments

I have incurred many personal intellectual debts while developing the theory presented here. My creditors include Peter Loptson, Thomas Hurka, John Campbell, Robert Young, Robert Fox, Alec Hyslop, Ross Phillips, Tim Oakley, the late David Lewis, John Bigelow, J.J.C. Smart, Andrew Moore, Rob Hudson, Emer O'Hagan, and others. In response to oral or written presentations of the ideas in this book, they pointed out errors that I hope I have corrected and presented challenges that I hope I have met. I am grateful to Gillian Lubansky for her help during the final stages. Finally, I wish to thank the readers for McGill-Queen's University Press, whose suggestions resulted in many improvements.

I developed a predecessor of this book while at La Trobe University. I am grateful to La Trobe and the Commonwealth of Australia for their support in the form of an Overseas Postgraduate Research Scholarship. Publication was made possible by subventions from the University of Saskatchewan's Publications Fund and Academic Participation and Professional Development Fund, and I am grateful for that support as well.

Introduction

My investigation of human morality was motivated by dissatisfaction with the theories presented to me when I was a student, not with the wonder that, in the traditional picture, motivates philosophers. I simply did not think that the theories explained their subject convincingly: they did not answer all the questions that I wanted answered in a way that satisfied me. I was therefore led, eventually, to conduct my own explorations. This is my report of those explorations. It is the presentation of a theory I call "evolutionary intuitionism" because it is evolutionary and because it has all the features of classical ethical intuitionism, except the property of being vulnerable to the objection that there is no way to distinguish reliable from unreliable intuitions. It is a theory about the origin of objective moral facts and how they influence human beings.

I believe that the explorations have been worthwhile, partly because the possible world in which evolutionary intuitionism is true might be the actual world (and I believe it is), partly because exploring that possible world might help to advance our understanding even if it is not actual, partly because that world is intrinsically interesting, and primarily because it is there and needed to be explored. The exploration is philosophical: I point out implications of the theory and examine them, try to solve problems that arise, and so on.

Evolutionary intuitionism suits my prejudices. It is important to me that human morality should turn out to be objective. Philosophers who do not strive to produce theories on which morality is objective have never, it seems to me, seriously contemplated the possibility of being oppressed or outcast. Societies can function quite well while denying moral equality to many and need not be inconsistent or hypocritical in doing so. But I do not believe that the individual exists for the sake of the group, the tribe, the state, or the species.

It is also important to me that accounts of human morality be compatible with the sciences and with evolutionary biology in particular. Some ethicists seem to think that almost anything can be built on the foundation that evolution provides, but they are mistaken. Our biological nature is not a neutral substratum that will support any moral theory at all and that can be ignored by ethicists. On the contrary, it limits the possibilities quite strictly. The surest way to avoid a conflict between a moral theory and our biological nature is to give the theory an evolutionary foundation. At any rate, theories that do not seriously acknowledge our biological nature as the best contemporary science portrays it and that do not include a demonstration of their compatibility with it are suspect for that reason alone.

Evolutionary intuitionism differs from sociobiology in that it is evolutionary but not adaptationist. Morality is not in itself an adaptation but the by-product of one. Evolutionary intuitionism is therefore quite unlike the evolutionary theories of ethics advanced by Darwin, Ruse, Alexander, and others. Consequently, the arguments for it are different. Unlike adaptationist evolutionary ethics, it relies primarily on individual selection. Kin selection and reciprocal altruism, which are central to contemporary adaptationist evolutionary ethics, have only a peripheral role here. It differs even in the kind of things it identifies as the moral. Hence, the standard objections to evolutionary ethics, that is, the objections to *adaptationist* evolutionary ethics, cannot be used against my theory.

Evolutionary intuitionism has greater scope than most theories. It encompasses meta-ethics, normative ethics, and moral motivation within an explanatory framework of the sort that is standard in the sciences. The theory enables us to make empirically testable predictions and passes the empirical tests it confronts.

Evolutionary intuitionism stands apart from all other moral theories. Different kinds of normative moral theories differ with respect to the kinds of properties of acts they regard as of primary moral significance. Roughly, consequentialism appeals to the consequences of acts, virtue theory to their antecedents, and deontology to their intrinsic properties. Evolutionary intuitionism fits nowhere in that taxonomy. Instead, it appeals to the relations of acts to another entity, as I shall explain in chapter 2. It is not just a new theory; it is also a new kind of theory.

In the first chapter, I set out to distinguish my project from the sorts of projects that adaptationist evolutionary ethicists work on. I argue that their projects are doomed to failure and that seeing why gives us some reason to think that the truth must be with an evolutionary by-product theory of the sort I advance here. The evolutionary improbability of most other theories gives us more reason to think so.

In the second chapter, I map out the basic elements of evolutionary intuitionism. Metaphorically, I set out the "axioms" of the "system." No doubt, some will see the "axioms" as odd and even bizarre. I think that this is a consequence of their unfamiliarity. What matters is how well they explain human morality, which cannot be determined on the basis of initial impressions.

Next, I set out an evolutionary explanation for the origin of the basic elements and point out some of the ways in which it differs from adaptationist accounts. The evolutionary explanation has empirical implications that are confirmed by observations – or, so I shall argue. Metaphorically, I prove my "axioms." Of course, what I actually succeed in doing will fall short of providing a logical proof.

In the three succeeding chapters, I explore the normative, motivational, and meta-ethical aspects of evolutionary intuitionism. Metaphorically, I examine the properties and implications of the "axioms." Normatively, the results are good enough. Motivationally, acting morally is the default option, but there are ways to avoid it. Moreover, there are factors that produce variation in moral codes even though they all have the same basis. Nonetheless, it is possible to distinguish reliable from unreliable intuitions. Meta-ethically, we get a standard sort of intuitionism. Realism, objectivism, and cognitivism all turn out to be true.

I conclude by evaluating the theory as an explanation of human morality. I do not go so far as to declare evolutionary intuitionism to be certainly true. For one thing, I do not compare it extensively enough with competing theories to make that claim; comparisons are made only by the way, on occasions when it is necessary or illuminating to indicate differences. Moreover, it is a novel theory, and it would be unwise to claim that there will never be a better one. It is always possible in principle for a scientific theory to be superseded by a better one, and it is my intention that this theory should be of the same kind as scientific theories in its appeal to empirical observations.

EVOLUTIONARY INTUITIONISM

I

Rejecting Adaptationism in Ethics

TWO KINDS OF EVOLUTIONARY ETHICS

Common usage of the label "evolutionary ethics" obscures the fact that there are two fundamentally and radically different possible types: adaptationist theories and by-product theories. Quite a lot of work has been done on the first type; little on the second. What people usually think of as evolutionary ethics is *adaptationist* evolutionary ethics. But this book is about a by-product theory that I call "evolutionary intuitionism" because it is ethical intuitionism with an evolutionary foundation. In order to clear the way for it and to avoid being associated with the sort of evolutionary ethics that many philosophers regard as disreputable, I will argue that adaptationist evolutionary ethics is unlikely to succeed.

There can be no reasonable doubt that the explanation for the human capacity for morality is fundamentally evolutionary. By that capacity, I mean either a range of innate moral beliefs and dispositions or a capacity to develop non-innate moral codes to govern our interactions with other human beings (at least) or a mixture of the two. The definition is disjunctive because I want to avoid making any assumptions about what variation and natural selection have actually produced. I will call the moral capacity referred to in the first disjunct a "complete capacity," that referred to in the second a "bare capacity," and that in the third a "mixed capacity."

Although there can be no doubt that our capacity for morality is fundamentally a product of evolution, there is good reason to doubt that it is adaptive. If it was, certain widespread moral beliefs should not exist and certain instances of what many take to be morally commendable behaviour should not occur. Specifically, the selection processes to which adaptationists appeal are not sufficient to produce moral agents with the capacity to believe or the inclination to act on the belief that it is particularly meritorious to help members of the human species who are outsiders relative to them. We should regard the Good Samaritan as contemptible, not inspirational.

Some think that we can readily extend our moral concern from insiders to outsiders and even to members of other species. Inspired by works like Peter Singer's *The Expanding Circle*, their intuition owes everything to metaphor and nothing to reason. It may seem to describe a natural progression, but in fact, nothing is more unnatural. Evolution does not create a neutral foundation that will support anything that we care to place on it. The selection processes will take us only in a direction of their choosing; they will get us as far as they can, and then, instead of letting us continue, they will work to prevent us from getting any further.

Proponents of adaptationist evolutionary ethics have grappled unsuccessfully with the Good Samaritan problem. The evolutionary selection processes they appeal to would tend to prevent Good Samaritans from coming into existence by producing people with incompatible dispositions. They would also tend to eliminate any Good Samaritans that happened to come into existence because Good Samaritanism is maladaptive. Moreover, adaptationist attempts to explain Good Samaritanism away have not been successful.

I will mostly ignore the possibility that our being moral agents is a random mutation or other chance phenomenon that natural selection will eliminate. Morality is too widespread, has existed for too long, and is too central to human life to be an aberration that will eventually vanish. Barring chance, if our moral capacity is ultimately evolutionary in origin and if morality is not adaptive, it must be the inseparable by-product of an adaptation.

In rejecting adaptationist evolutionary ethics, I do not intend to endorse broader attacks on adaptationism.[1] I tend to agree with Ernst Mayr that "the principal reason for [taking an adaptationist approach] is its great heuristic value."[2] Methodologically, we should usually first try to discover an adaptationist explanation. When we know that adaptationist explanations are unlikely to succeed, however, we should turn our attention to possible by-product explanations. Whatever the best policy might be, there may be true adaptationist explanations in some cases and true by-product explanations in others, and we may be able to find evidence for or against them.

AN INSIGHT, AN INTUITION, AND AN ASSUMPTION

All adaptationist theories, including the work of Darwin himself,[3] of Michael Ruse,[4] and of many others, recognize a fundamental fact of evolution, accept a basic moral intuition, and make a basic assumption. The same three factors must inspire any adaptationist explanation of our moral capacity.

The fundamental fact is that if the individual organism is "the exclusive unit of selection, then natural selection works *against* the evolution of altruism," because it would not be adaptive.[5] Biological altruism is any sort of behaviour that increases the fitness of other organisms at a fitness cost to the altruistic organism. The altruistic organism does something that on average increases the viability or fertility of other organisms but that impairs its own viability or fertility. Biologically altruistic organisms tend to be eliminated. Non-altruistic organisms, on the other hand, may receive the benefits but incur none of the costs and are more likely to succeed in reproducing if they do. "'Look out for Number One' should be Mother Nature's first and only rule."[6] As for the intuition, it is that some morally laudable acts are biologically altruistic. The set of morally laudable acts and the set of biologically altruistic acts intersect. Certainly, acting in a morally praiseworthy way does sometimes mean that the moral agent will reduce his own fitness. For instance, raising an unrelated orphan reduces fitness because doing so uses up resources that could be used to raise the foster parent's own offspring. Finally, the assumption is that the human moral capacity is biologically adaptive, if not actually an adaptation. It is assumed to exist because it increases our viability or fertility.

The fact, the intuition, and the assumption determine the nature of adaptationist ethics. If morality is an adaptation and if the supreme moral principle is not that all individuals ought to maximize their genetic legacy through individual selection, then morality must be the product of some selection process other than individual selection. The other available processes are group selection, kin selection, and reciprocal altruism. Group selection occurs when there is selection for a feature of an organism because the feature confers an advantage on the group to which the organism belongs. Kin selection occurs when there is selection for a feature because it confers an advantage on the organism's kin. Both processes can work because the organism shares its genes with others. When organisms share a gene, the organisms in question possess distinct tokens of the same type of gene – just as different people, for example, may possess different copies (tokens) of the same book (type). What counts as success is increasing the number of tokens of a type of gene in succeeding generations no matter how the increase is achieved. Successful genes become "best sellers" no matter what "marketing techniques" they have to use.

Reciprocal altruism occurs when an organism benefits another in the "expectation" that it will receive benefits in return: the "expectation" need not be conscious. Because of the mutual aid, which is typically provided at low cost for considerably greater benefits, interacting reciprocal altruists are fitter than competitors who do not engage in reciprocal altruism. For example, people who give directions to strangers incur a small cost and save the strangers the much greater search costs. Individuals belonging to groups whose members help each other in such ways can gain a great deal.

Given the fact, the intuition and the assumption, there is no alternative but to appeal to one or another of the three processes in order to explain ethics in adaptationist terms. The orthodox view since the 1960s[7] has been that group selection is possible but that the circumstances in which it could occur are so rare that we can ignore the possibility. The circumstances are rare because groups would have to be unrealistically isolated from each other. The orthodox view leads some to conclude that its reliance on group selection poses a problem for nineteenth-century evolutionary ethics.[8] In contrast, contemporary sociobiology appeals to kin selection and reciprocal altruism, which the orthodox view does not regard as forms of group selection. Nonetheless, group selection does have its defenders. Elliott Sober and David Sloan Wilson have recently attempted to rehabilitate it.[9] Naturally, I cannot ignore group selection if I am to eliminate all possible adaptationist explanations of our moral capacity as improbable. However, I want to avoid the controversies surrounding it. Therefore, I will assume that the adaptationist affirms the following disjunction: the human capacity for morality is the evolutionary product of group selection, kin selection, or reciprocal altruism. The "or" is inclusive, so the three processes could combine in various ways. I do not assume that only one process is involved or that all of them are. As far as my argument here is concerned, the dispute over whether group selection occurs in some cases will be irrelevant. In the next section, I will present some observations that we should not make if *any* adaptationist account of morality were true. I will set out in detail why we should not expect to make them in the section after that.

RECALCITRANT OBSERVATIONS

Adaptationism has difficulty explaining our apparent ability to believe that all other human moral agents are worthy of moral consideration no matter the community to which they belong. It is not merely a matter of moral intuitions. Adaptationism confronts observations. The most important is that *some people act as though all others are worthy of moral consideration.* For instance, some people who rescued Jews from Nazis certainly did so. It was irrelevant to them that the Jews were members of another group, were not kin, and were not – and could not be expected to become – partners in reciprocally altruistic relationships. Furthermore, a far greater number recognize and accept that the rescuers acted in a morally laudable way. So, the second recalcitrant observation is that *many people approve of those who act as though all others are worthy of moral consideration.* Finally, people tend to regard those who act as though all others are worthy of moral consideration as especially praiseworthy *because* they go to the aid of members of an alien group, *because* they help non-kin, and *because* they do not expect gain, reward, or reciprocation. Many people do not regard Good Samaritans as perverse but as particularly virtuous. With respect to those who rescued Jews, Martin Gilbert writes that "long after the Righteous of the Second World War have died, they will serve as models of the best in human behaviour and achievement to which anyone may choose to aspire."[10]

The phenomena are undeniable. Consider the Ukrainians who tried to save Jews from Nazis. Ukrainians and Jews were two ethnically, religiously, and socio-economically distinct groups that shared the same territory and that had a history of mutual animosity. Both groups regarded themselves as distinct; there was little intermarriage between them. Most helpers aided strangers.[11] Being aware of the situation under Nazi occupation, the probable fate of the Jews, and the dangers to themselves, they could not have reasonably anticipated future gain of any sort, let alone gain proportionate to their risk.[12] The dangers were clear and extreme. "Unlike in most countries occupied by the Nazis, in Ukraine and Poland assisting Jews was punishable by death."[13] "Indeed, about 100 Ukrainians from all the strata of the population were executed by the Germans in eastern Galicia due to their attempts to hide Jews."[14] Even worse, "in the Reichskommissariat Ukraine the Nazis could and did kill not only the 'guilty ones,' but also their children."[15] Hanging families was consistent with the Nazi goal of reducing the total "subhuman" Slavic population to a "manageable" thirty million, who could be used as slaves.[16] In contrast, "in the 'Germanic' Netherlands, the people who helped Anne Frank hide were not even arrested."[17] The actions of Ukrainian rescuers were therefore actually or potentially biologically altruistic.

It would be going too far to say that the people whose families were executed along with them were immorally reckless. The exculpatory factor is that most rescuers believed that they could get away with it; their efforts were contingent on that belief.[18] Some rescuers were tragically wrong, but even if they should have known better, their error is surely forgivable. Moreover, helping Jews was biologically altruistic even when the death penalty was not imposed. Rescuers still had to care for strangers at a significant cost to themselves in terms of energy and resources, which increased the probability of the rescuers dying from starvation or disease.

At any rate, as I shall argue in the next section, if the human capacity for morality could be explained by group selection, kin selection, or reciprocal altruism, there should have been no Ukrainian rescuers. Moreover, if our moral capacity could be explained by the three processes to which adaptationism appeals, we should not approve of their actions. But approval is widespread, particularly because the rescuers were helping people who were unrelated to them in any of the ways that adaptationism considers significant. From an adaptationist perspective, the people we should admire are those who deceived Jews by pretending to be willing to help them, who took their valuables, and who threatened to turn them over to the Nazis if they did not leave.[19] But, surely, not even adaptationists can bring themselves to accept this implication of their approach.

Michael Ruse tries to deny the observations. "We certainly pay lip service to our need to respect members of remote and foreign cultures as ends in themselves; but, whether we really truly believe that we have a moral obligation to them, is, I think, a very debatable point."[20] In fact, there can be no reasonable doubt that some people believe that we ought to help outsiders. The fact that others apparently do not believe it does not mean that no one does, and the existence of the believing subset of humanity is enough to falsify adaptationist explanations of our moral capacity. Moreover, if an adaptationist explanation of our moral capacity were true, our paying lip service to the obligation would itself be peculiar and unexpected. I do not deny that many people hate outsiders and are willing to exploit them, that others are indifferent to them, or that yet others have preferences that outweigh any desire they might have to help them. My point is that such people are not the only people. Moreover, the antagonistic and the indifferent are usually intellectually and morally on the defensive. That would be surprising if adaptationism explained our moral capacity.

In what amounts to a diversion, Ruse mentions Jesus, Mother Teresa, and Gandhi, commenting that "most of us admire saints, but feel no great pressure to follow them – nor do we think we should."[21] But rescuers were not messiahs or mystics. They were ordinary people in extraordinary circumstances who tried to save fellow human beings. The morally sensitive would feel tremendous pressure to be rescuers if they were in the same circumstances. They would definitely think that they should even if they lacked the requisite courage. Ruse's comments on a few highly religious individuals do not put the recalcitrant observations in doubt.

Ruse tries to soft-pedal the implications of his view. He claims that we will feel an obligation to help outsiders but that we will feel a much stronger obligation to help insiders. His position is that "the Darwinian expects a stronger sense of moral obligation to those who are in the same moral pool as we, than to others."[22] "We have a moral obligation to promote happiness, but this obligation weakens as the circle widens."[23] Obviously, Ruse is appealing to the "expanding circle" of Peter Singer. In fact, Ruse does not try to justify his contention that we will feel an obligation towards outsiders. Nor does he argue that there will be no outsiders. He does suggest that some people will be morally more sensitive than others, but as long as he does not show that there are no complete outsiders or, alternatively, as long as he does not explain in adaptationist terms why we would be morally sensitive to outsiders to any degree at all, he begs the question. When he declares that "no one is saying that there are humans towards whom we have no sense of obligation whatsoever,"[24] he fails to see that if adaptationism did explain our moral capacity, there not only could be but also probably would be people with respect to whom we would have no sense of obligation at all.

Adaptationist ethics is on a slippery slope. If some behaviour that promotes fitness counts as morally acceptable, there is no reason why all does not. But counting all such behaviour as moral would result in an ethical naturalism that simply equated the good with what increases fitness. The two are not the same. We need some principled way to distinguish the moral from the non-moral, but adaptationism cannot provide it. Some commentators explicitly identify the moral with the pro-social at the outset,[25] but they may be begging the question. If pro-social behaviour is identical with or subsumes moral behaviour, then our moral capacity will probably have to be produced by some combination of the three processes to which adaptationism appeals. The danger is that our moral capacity will end up being implicitly defined as whatever adaptationism can explain and wants to label as our moral capacity. The outcome could be that adaptationism starts with a range of behaviour and beliefs that we intuitively regard as moral, apparently explains some of the phenomena, and retroactively declares what it has not explained to be non-moral or non-existent. Ruse's arguments exemplify the danger.

WHY ADAPTATIONIST PROCESSES PROMOTE PARTIALITY

There are good evolutionary reasons why we should not expect group selection, kin selection, or reciprocal altruism to give us a complete or mixed moral capacity that makes no distinctions among different segments of humanity. There are good evolutionary reasons why we should not expect them to lead directly to a disposition to be a Good Samaritan or directly to a belief that people ought to be Good Samaritans. As indicated earlier, the problem is not merely that the selection processes would not be powerful enough. It is also that they would tend to counteract and prevent the development of the requisite dispositions or beliefs and to eliminate them if they did arise. As Stephen Jay Gould puts it, "strongly *in*adaptive features hold little prospect for an evolutionary legacy because natural selection must soon eliminate them."[26] The problem is not one of explaining cases of supererogation but of understanding why people advocate and approve of what they would almost certainly regard as *wrong* if adaptationism explained their moral capacity.

In the case of group and kin selection, we should expect people to be able to distinguish insiders from outsiders, to treat insiders better than outsiders, and in fact to be willing in principle to exploit outsiders for the sake of insiders. "Group selection does provide a setting in which helping behavior directed at members of one's own group can evolve; however, it equally provides a context in which hurting members in other groups can be selectively advantageous. Group selection favors within-group niceness *and* between-group nastiness."[27] In the case of Ukrainians and Jews, it would favour the former robbing the latter and sending them on their way. Kin selection should do the same thing. "Parental care is a behavior that most people find pleasing ... However, if selection promotes an altruistic concern for the welfare of one's near and dear, it may also promote indifference or malevolence toward outsiders."[28] The fact that families are frequently nice to their own members but not especially nasty to other families is not necessarily counter-evidence. If group selection occurs, "conflict and competition are not eliminated but merely elevated in the biological hierarchy, where the problem of social dilemmas appears all over again at an even grander (and potentially more destructive) scale."[29]

At any rate, if people did not distinguish between insiders and outsiders and if they did not favour insiders, *there would be nothing on which the selection processes could get a causal grip*. The operation of those processes *requires* that we make the distinction and *requires* that we be partial. Hence, the selection processes of adaptationist evolutionary ethics cannot produce a disposition to help outsiders or a belief that one ought to do so, and if either were to arise by some accident, the same selection processes would tend to eliminate it.

It is obvious that people are good at distinguishing between insiders and outsiders and that they often prefer the interests of the former to the latter. We can identify our kin far more often than not. We favour them equally frequently. There is often invidious discrimination within societies. Nationalism and sectarianism are common. Nor is this sort of thing something new. People were clearly good at distinguishing insiders from outsiders in the environment of evolutionary adaptation.

As for reciprocal altruism, the average fitness costs of helping must be less than the average fitness benefits received by the helper. Moreover, people must be able to distinguish between cases in which the costs are too high and those in which the costs are acceptable. Individuals who could not make the distinction or who did not act accordingly would be less fit than those who could and did. The former would be exploited by the latter and ultimately displaced by them. As R.L. Trivers puts it, "if the cost/benefit ratio is an important parameter in determining the adaptiveness of reciprocal altruism, then humans should be selected to be sensitive to the cost and benefit of an altruistic act, both in deciding whether to perform one and in deciding whether, or how much, to reciprocate."[30] In the case of Ukrainian rescuers of Jews, the calculations should have resulted in the Jews not being helped at all. The rescuers could calculate not just the danger of being hanged by the Nazis but also the costs of feeding, clothing, and housing the rescued.

According to Trivers, reciprocal altruism is promoted when there are many opportunities for reciprocation, when there are repeated interactions with the same individuals, and when "pairs of altruists are exposed 'symmetrically' to altruistic situations, that is, in such a way that the two are able to render roughly equivalent benefits to each other at roughly equivalent costs."[31] None of the conditions held in the case of Jews and rescuers. These were predominantly one-off situations, and a rescuer could not reasonably anticipate being the rescued in the future. If rescuers had all been motivated by inclinations that were selected for by reciprocal altruism, we would expect them to have anticipated future gains and to have been disappointed, even bitter, when they did not get them. But they were not. Like group and kin selection, reciprocal altruism will get us so far and no further. It too is a self-limiting causal process.

Richard Alexander argues that morality is produced by what he calls "indirect reciprocity," which "is what happens when direct reciprocity occurs in the presence of an interested audience."[32] According to Alexander, "returns ... may take at least three major forms: (1) the beneficent individual may later be engaged in profitable interactions by individuals who have observed his behavior ... (2) the beneficent individual may be rewarded with direct compensation ... or (3) the beneficent individual may be rewarded by ... the success of the group."[33] Naturally, anyone can play this game: participants need not be kin or members of the same ethnic or religious group. Of course, that there are no necessary limits to group membership does not mean that there will be a single group of indirect reciprocators. Competition between groups and barriers to co-operation between them would almost inevitably prevent its development. There does not appear to be a single, worldwide group now and even if there were, there would be no guarantee that it would persist for very long. Indirect reciprocity is therefore unlikely to erase the distinction between insiders and outsiders.

Whether we belong to a single group or not, indirect reciprocity cannot explain all the help extended to Jews by Ukrainians. For one thing, there could not have been an interested audience for obvious reasons. Moreover, self-advertisement would have been inconsistent with the modest and self-effacing nature of rescuers.[34] For another, many rescuers did not expect and did not receive direct compensation. Nor did their efforts benefit the group to which they belonged. Finally, "if current views of evolutionary processes are correct, reciprocity flourishes when donated benefits are relatively inexpensive compared to the returns,"[35] but that sort of ratio did not hold in this case. In other words, indirect reciprocity would not produce a moral capacity that enabled people to give more than they could possibly gain in return. There may be no necessary limits with respect to potential beneficiaries but there are still limits to how much the altruist will do for those beneficiaries. The Ukrainians would have been prevented from helping Jews.

Of course, we may be dealing with a biological counterpart to rule utilitarianism rather than act utilitarianism.[36] Instead of considering actions on a case-by-case basis as we would if we were act ultilitarians, let us suppose, in keeping with rule utilitarianism, that there has been selection for people who act consistently in virtuous ways. On this view, Ukrainians helping Jews would have been following a rule that, on average, had been advantageous for their ancestors. They would have been trying to save others because they were descended from people who did not calculate the cost of saving particular individuals in particular cases but followed a general rule of saving others. And we would approve of their actions because we would have the same evolutionary history. Now, it is certainly true that in many environments, consistently adhering to a rule to treat others fairly, for instance, is a better strategy than deciding whether to treat them fairly on a case-by-case basis. The problem is that in most cases there seems to be no reason why a human being would care as much for his reputation among outsiders as he would among insiders and no reason, therefore, why he would apply the rule to outsiders. In the environment of evolutionary adaptation, the only plausible exceptions would have been when he wished to maintain his reputation as a dangerous foe or as a reliable ally. The question would still remain, however, why some people concern themselves with their reputation among outsiders who are neither enemies nor potential allies. The dispositions that have been hypothesized do not explain why they do.

At best, then, adaptationism replaces "egoism" with "tribalism." This may be progress. Darwin thought so. Robert J. Richards comments that Darwin "preserved a conception of man as an intrinsically moral being, a being whose morality tinctured the very core of his substance. Certainly, human beings acted selfishly on occasion. Darwin nonetheless believed that men could recognize the needs of others and could respond unselfishly to satisfy those needs."[37] But for Darwin, as Richards makes clear, we recognize the needs of others and respond unselfishly to them because the others in question are members of the same community that we belong to. Darwin's position is still incompatible with the notion that it is particularly virtuous to aid the complete outsider. On the contrary, "if one consistently adhered to the Darwinist canon, the logical social ethic (beyond being merely egocentric) would be to join with genetically kindred persons to get the better, reproductively, of all others, ultimately to replace them by whatever means available."[38] Since adaptationism cannot produce dispositions to do any more than that or beliefs that we ought to do any more than that, adaptationism cannot explain the Good Samaritan observations.

THE APPEAL TO MISFIRING

If adaptationism cannot explain Good Samaritanism, it must try to *explain it away.* The help given to outsiders has to be a mistake or misfiring.[39] In this section, I will argue that the adaptationist cannot explain Good Samaritanism away if our capacity for morality is a complete or mixed capacity (as defined in the first section of this chapter) and if Good Samaritanism has a specifically biological origin. In the next, I will argue that the adaptationist cannot explain it away if our capacity is a bare capacity (as also defined in the first section of this chapter) and if Good Samaritanism per se has a non-biological origin. It is unnecessary to discuss complete and mixed capacities separately, because the discussion concerns not the whole of human morality but merely the Good Samaritan observations. As far as the present discussion goes, if our moral capacity is mixed (that is, partly innate and partly the result of non-innate moral codes), then Good Samaritanism is in the biological, not the non-biological, part of the mix.

If the human moral capacity is either complete or mixed and if Good Samaritanism has a specifically biological explanation, the adaptationist needs an explanation analogous to the one for some cases in which people are uninterested in suitable sexual partners, as happens on some Israeli kibbutzim. Sociobiologists explain this phenomenon in terms of an ultimate evolutionary aim, a proximate mechanism for the achievement of the aim, and an abnormal situation in which the proximate mechanism misfires. In the example just mentioned, the ultimate aim is incest avoidance, the proximate mechanism is to become sexually uninterested in people with whom one has been raised, and the abnormal situation is that unrelated children are raised together.[40] The evolutionary advantages of the ultimate aim are uncontroversial, and it is obvious why the proximate mechanism would work effectively enough. It is clear why there would be selection for a rule of thumb rather than a mechanism that enabled humans to detect their kin unerringly – the rule of thumb is far less costly to follow, and it works well enough most of the time. And, finally, it is clear why there would be misfires in the case of children raised together on a kibbutz.

There is nothing similar in the case of the human capacity for morality. First, it is not obvious and uncontroversial that the function of morality is to advance the interests of some sort of in-group. Adaptationism *assumes* that the human moral capacity is adaptive or an adaptation. There is no independent evidence for the assumption. On the contrary, there is evidence that supports the view that it is false – as argued in the previous section, the adaptationist selection processes cannot produce Good Samaritanism. Since we lack independent evidence for it and since by-product explanations are also possible, the adaptationist assumption that morality is adaptive is an *arbitrary* assumption.

Second, there is no uncontroversial rule of thumb that would enable people to achieve the end in most cases but that would be susceptible to misfiring. As long as it assumes that the human capacity for morality is adaptive, adaptationism requires an auxiliary hypothesis to explain away the observation that people sometimes help outsiders. But since, as we have just seen, it is arbitrary to assume that the human capacity for morality is adaptive, it is also arbitrary to assume that helping outsiders results from misfiring rather than being the right thing to do.

Third, it is not clear that there have ever been abnormal situations in which misfires could occur. In order for us to have evolved in such a way that the misfire would occur when we were confronted by an outsider, we would have to mistake the outsider for an insider. For that error to occur, it would have to be the case that our evolution took place in isolated groups. If the groups had not been isolated, there would have been selection for the ability to distinguish insiders from outsiders and hence, selection for the elimination of the misfires: it would always be in the interest of insiders to avoid bestowing benefits on outsiders. Group selection has been regarded as implausible because it would require an unreasonable degree of isolation, but adaptationism requires at least the same degree of isolation if it is going to explain why many people regard it as a good thing to help outsiders.

Not only does adaptationism have trouble explaining away the first two Good Samaritan observations, it cannot even attempt to explain the third. From an adaptationist perspective, it is bizarre that anyone would regard those who help outsiders as especially virtuous. The approval cannot be the result of mistaking outsiders for insiders. On the contrary, the approver must correctly identify outsiders as outsiders. The fact that significant numbers of people believe that aiding outsiders is extraordinarily meritorious is evidence for the contention that adaptationist explanations of human morality are false, because those who approved would be less fit than those who withheld approval. They would be less fit because they would be more likely to be Good Samaritans themselves.

Of course, in some situations it can be advantageous for outsiders to promote themselves as insiders and to be taken by insiders to be other insiders. Adopted orphans fare better than abandoned ones. Those who promote "the brotherhood of man" can gain when others accept their teachings and consequently treat them better than they would otherwise. There is no need to think that the self-promotion need even be conscious. Individuals that got treated as insiders when they were really outsiders would simply be fitter and would tend to pass on their capacity to "deceive." Of course, they would not have things all their own way. There would be an arms race with real insiders developing a better capacity to detect and reject pseudo-insiders. Adaptationists might try to explain away the Good Samaritan observations by hypothesizing that Good Samaritans are simply losers in the arms race. But this is not evidence that the function of morality is to advance the interests of insiders, that there is a rule of thumb that can result in misfiring, or that we ever lived in environments in which a rule of thumb could evolve. Moreover, an arms race would not explain why some people regard those who help outsiders as especially virtuous. This kind of explanation helps preserve adaptationism from falsification in an ad hoc fashion. But the explanation does not show that any version of adaptationist evolutionary ethics is true.

THE IMPOTENCE OF CULTURE AND REASON

If adaptationism gave us a bare capacity for morality, something else would have to transform us into Good Samaritans. The idea is usually that evolution would take us part of the way and that culture or reason would take us the rest of the way. The trouble is that Good Samaritanism would still be maladaptive. If our bare capacity can be explained in adaptationist terms, then it exists because the ability to develop a moral code makes us fitter. However, if the ability to develop a moral code is to make us fitter, then moral codes themselves must typically improve fitness. Any moral code, or part of a code, that reduces fitness is therefore maladaptive. The problem is to explain how a maladaptive moral code could originate and persist. Unfortunately for adaptationism, neither culture nor reason can explain the origin and persistence of Good Samaritanism.

Robert Boyd and Peter Richerson posit the existence of a conformist bias to help explain the influence of culture, arguing that a tendency to behave in the same way as others in the group is an adaptation.[41] They show how this bias can lead to stable altruism. Altruistic groups do better than non-altruistic ones and non-altruists cannot subvert altruistic groups because, when they join the group, their conformist bias leads them to act altruistically. Boyd and

Richerson's account is preferable to other explanations of cultural phenomena in that it explains not only how they come into existence but also why they do.[42] It is preferable to accounts that show how culture can promote an outcome when people find it attractive but that cannot explain why people find it attractive.[43] Nonetheless, once again, this account gives us no reason to expect that members of altruistic groups would help non-members. They would still distinguish insiders from outsiders and would still favour insiders.

Boyd and Richerson argue that reward and punishment can promote any kind of behaviour,[44] a position endorsed by Sober and Wilson: "In Boyd and Richerson's theory, within-group selection can promote virtually *any* set of primary behaviors, depending on the social norms ... The costs and benefits of the primary behaviors simply become irrelevant when they are overwhelmed by the rewards and punishments associated with social norms."[45] Sober and Wilson "suggest that low-cost secondary behaviors" – acts of rewarding or punishing others – "play a crucial role in the creation and maintenance of diversity in primary behaviors, which are nonfunctional outside the context of the cultural system."[46] The primary behaviours transform groups of people into adaptive units: they exist because they do so.

However, this kind of explanation cannot explain all the aid extended to Jews by Ukrainians. The threat of capital punishment should have overwhelmed any desire to help and should have led to a new social norm. Moreover, if the explanation were correct, then the helpers would have been the most conservative and conformist Ukrainians. They would have been very strongly committed to the old ways and unable to change quickly in response to the new circumstances. Instead, the characteristics of rescuers included "individuality, or an inability to blend into their social environment"[47] and "independence or self-reliance, a willingness to act in accordance with personal convictions, regardless of how those convictions were viewed by others."[48] It was nonconformists, not conformists, who were most likely to become rescuers.

A further problem for this sort of explanation is that almost all the rescuers said they had done "the only thing a decent person would do."[49] If Ukrainian rescuers had acted in response to cultural norms, one would have expected them to say that they did what any decent Ukrainian would do. Instead, they typically referred to their humanity rather than their nationality. This would be surprising if their actions had been inspired by their culture.

Boyd and Richerson also posit what they call "prestige bias." According to them, prestige bias is a form of "success bias," the tendency to imitate the successful. Apparently, it "can lead to an unstable, runaway process much like the one that may give rise to exaggerated characteristics such as peacock tails."[50] Prestige bias might explain the motivation of some Christian rescuers. For Christians, no one would have more prestige than Jesus Christ, who advocated the love of others and who declared that the greatest possible love was demonstrated by giving up one's life for others. However, there were also Chinese, Japanese, and Turkish rescuers, and their motivation probably cannot be explained in this way.[51] Moreover, prestige bias does not explain why those who help outsiders would ever come to be admired. There are good evolutionary reasons to think that helping outsiders would never become prestigious. An appeal to prestige bias would be yet another ad hoc way of preserving adaptationism from falsification by the Good Samaritan observations.

Some people believe that culture enables us to transcend our biological origins. It does not. In the absence of an evolutionary explanation for culture like Boyd and Richerson's – that is, if culture were "superorganic" – the most that would be true would be that organisms that evolved in one environment could fail to flourish in another. Adaptations to an old environment can be liabilities in a new one: moths were fitter when there were no electric lights. Cultural changes are changes in the environment. They can affect human fitness just as electric light affects the fitness of moths. The only difference between the effect of electric light on moths and that of culture on us is that we ourselves create the changes in our environment that we call "culture." The difference is of no theoretical significance. Organisms that do things that affect other organisms of the same species are simply part of the environment of the affected organisms. Our dispositions would be ones that were selected for because they enabled our ancestors to reproduce more successfully than others in the environment they inhabited at the time. But the same dispositions would not necessarily promote fitness in the environment we inhabit now: they might just make it look as though we were no longer governed by our biology. Helping outsiders would still be maladaptive. In fact, those who appeal to the existence of old dispositions in new environments simply take us back to the kind of misfiring "explanation" discussed in the previous section.

Francisco J. Ayala holds that morality is a cultural superstructure raised upon a biological substructure. The latter is the bare capacity and the former the content. Specifically, he claims that "the three necessary, and jointly sufficient, conditions for ethical behavior ... are: (i) the ability to anticipate the consequences of one's own actions; (ii) the ability to make value judgments; and (iii) the ability to choose between alternative courses of action."[52] The conditions may be necessary, but they are obviously not sufficient, because the existence of an ability does not entail that it will be exercised. That issue aside, Ayala argues that although moral norms may increase, decrease, or have no effect on fitness, "discrepancies between accepted moral rules and biological survival are ... necessarily limited in scope or would otherwise lead to the extinction of the groups accepting such discrepant rules."[53] In other words, on Ayala's view, some misfires are theoretically permissible. Still, his account cannot describe Good Samaritanism except as maladaptive. It would be too discrepant. The abilities to foresee, value and choose should lead biological organisms to choose not to help outsiders.

Another possibility is that reason is an adaptation, that moral truths are truths of reason, and that the notion that it is especially meritorious to help outsiders is therefore a truth of reason.[54] The idea is that we became rational because rationality makes us fitter, but rationality makes us ethical as well – at least occasionally to our evolutionary detriment. However, there is a major problem with this possibility. It would be necessary for us to reason to the conclusion that it was good for insiders to help outsiders. The trouble is that people could always object that their intuitive conviction that they did not have to help outsiders proved that some of the assumptions with which the reasoning began were false. If some truths were inimical to evolutionary success, the adaptationist selection processes might blind us to them. There might be selection for us not to see that it is our humanity that makes us worthy of moral consideration and to believe instead that it is our being "Aryan," say. In fact, this is a common sort of "justification" for partiality: more than one nation has developed a master race syndrome. Hence, if morality were simply a matter of reason and if our ability to reason were an adaptation, it would be biologically possible – even easy – to avoid Good Samaritanism.

Moreover, it is implausible that reason would be the enemy of adaptationism rather than its ally. There is no reason why rationality should not be the slave of our evolutionary passions. If helping outsiders is maladaptive, then it is detrimental, and it ought to be possible to persuade people that it is. If we can learn to overcome our aversion to bitter substances because we know that they have medicinal benefits, surely we could learn to avoid performing detrimental acts.[55] In other words, if adaptationism were true and if reason had any influence on human morality, there would be as much reason to think that it would promote the elimination of Good Samaritanism as there is to think that it would work for its preservation. All in all, adaptationist appeals to culture or reason to explain Good Samaritanism are just so much hand-waving.

BY-PRODUCT THEORIES AND EVOLUTIONARY INTUITIONISM

The observations that have served as a touchstone in this chapter are that some people help outsiders, that others approve of their actions, and that the people who do help outsiders are regarded as especially virtuous. There are many reasonable, intelligent, and morally decent people who cannot be convinced that helping outsiders is a mistake. They cannot be convinced that the Ukrainians who rescued Jews should have emulated the Ukrainians who robbed them and turned them out. They even regard the implication that the latter are not villains as a reason to reject adaptationist evolutionary ethics. Their reaction strongly supports the idea that helping outsiders is sometimes simply the right thing to do. The problem is to explain why it is right. As we have seen, the resources of adaptationist ethics are unable either to explain the observations or to explain them away.

There are no completely non-evolutionary options because, as Ayala argues, a non-evolutionary element must rest on an evolutionary foundation. If an evolutionary foundation is not the immediate basis for our moral capacity, then it must provide the substructure for the basis. This conclusion follows from the fact that we are products of evolution. Since adaptationism cannot accommodate Good Samaritanism, we are forced to conclude that our moral capacity is probably fundamentally an evolutionary by-product that is inextricably linked to an adaptation. If it were not, the maladaptiveness of Good Samaritanism would result in its elimination.

By-product theories cannot show that morality increases fitness, but they can explain Good Samaritanism without categorizing it as a moral mistake. The by-product of an adaptation is a feature that exists because it is tied to the adaptation. There is selection *for* the adaptation but selection *of* the by-product.[56] If the by-product itself reduces fitness, it persists as long as it cannot be separated from the adaptation that compensates for its negative effect. The adaptation without the by-product would increase fitness more than the adaptation with the by-product does, but the combination still increases fitness. To put the point more generally, if the selection processes create anything that counteracts their own thrust in the long run, it must be the by-product of an adaptation that is inseparable from it. For example, in human beings, very big brains are presumably an adaptation. One by-product is a larger, more vulnerable skull that makes childbirth more difficult and dangerous, given the pelvic narrowing that is a by-product of bipedalism, another adaptation. Obviously, we cannot get bigger brains without getting bigger heads: the by-product is inseparable from the adaptation. There was selection *for* bigger brains but selection *of* larger heads.

Let us assume, then, that our bare moral capacity is an evolutionary by-product. There are four basic possibilities for the moral content, as distinct from the bare capacity: either it is an evolutionary adaptation, or it is a product of culture, or it is a product of reason, or it is also an evolutionary by-product. As for the first alternative, there will no selection for Good Samaritanism; there will in fact be selection for characteristics that would prevent it. And there would be selection for its elimination if it ever occurred by chance. It will again prove impossible for the adaptationist to explain it away. As for the second alternative, its origin would be a maladaptive accident from an evolutionary point of view, and there would be selection for its prevention and elimination. It is possible but improbable; it would be a temporary aberration. As for the third alternative, there are no grounds for thinking that reason would be in conflict with our biology with respect to Good Samaritanism. If it were, it would be the loser; and even before it was eliminated evolutionarily, we would be able to learn to overcome our inclination to become Good Samaritans. In short, all the problems pointed out in connection with adaptationism would recur in this new context. Hence, if our bare moral capacity is a by-product and if we want to explain Good Samaritanism, the relevant content of morality almost certainly has to be an evolutionary by-product as well. Therefore, if Good Samaritans deserve praise rather than derision, it is probable that the human capacity for morality is a by-product and that the by-product is a complete or mixed capacity in the sense set out at the beginning of this chapter.

Evolutionary intuitionism enables us to maintain that Good Samaritanism is not a mistake, as we shall see. But it explains more than Good Samaritanism, of course. It gives us grounds to accept a wide range of other moral judgments as well. It may not explain the whole of ethics but it accounts for a great deal. I turn, then, to the development of evolutionary intuitionism. If what I have argued so far is correct, evolutionary intuitionism is in the area where we can expect to find the truth about human morality. What follows is mostly evidence that it is in fact true.

2

The Design of Intuitionistic Organisms

ETHICAL INTUITIONISM ON AN EVOLUTIONARY BASIS

Moral agents, a moral community, and objective moral facts can come into existence in a possible world that is initially devoid of them and in which human beings are biological organisms and products of evolution by variation and natural selection. The transformation makes a form of ethical intuitionism true. By ethical intuitionism, I mean the meta-ethical position that includes the following claims.[1] First, moral realism is true. In other words, there are moral facts. A moral fact is a fact that would make true a moral judgment such as "It is wrong to torture the innocent." Second, objectivism is true. The moral facts are the same for all moral agents, and this is not an accident. In relevantly similar situations, the permissions and obligations of any two moral agents would be the same. Third, cognitivism is true: the moral facts are knowable. Fourth, since there are moral facts and since they are knowable, our moral judgments can be true. Error theories are therefore false. Fifth, the is/ought gap is unbridgeable. True moral judgments are not deducible from purely factual propositions. Sixth, morality is not instrumental. It may be useful, but that is not why it exists. Seventh, moral agents can be motivated to act in a morally acceptable manner without an extrinsic pay-off. We may have reasons to act morally even though doing so does not benefit us materially. Finally, we have intuitive access to moral truths, and consequently we can know what is right intuitively under certain conditions. In this world, intuitionism overcomes the difficulty that has resulted in the doctrine's widespread rejection, namely, the lack of a way to distinguish reliable from unreliable intuitions.

The description of the possible world constitutes an explanation of human morality, an explanation in the same sense that a scientific theory is an explanation. There is an evolutionary explanation for the origin of both the moral facts and the moral agents who intuit and are moved by them. Being both evolutionary and intuitionist, evolutionary intuitionism combines an unorthodox substructure with an orthodox and conservative superstructure. The rest of this chapter is devoted to explicating the elements of the theory and to showing how they result in moral agents, a moral community, and moral facts.

A NATURALLY SELECTED FOUNDATION FOR MORALITY

I am going to have to introduce some theoretical entities and some technical terms. The most important theoretical entity is a belief-like propositional attitude that is not a belief. I will call it a "foundational attitude," because it is a propositional attitude – just as beliefs, desires, hopes, fears and so on, are – and because it has a foundational role in evolutionary intuitionism.

As I have said, a foundational attitude is belief-like, but is not a belief. Unlike a belief, it is not meant to be an accurate representation of any aspect of the world. As we shall see, there was natural selection for foundational attitudes for reasons that had nothing to do with representational accuracy. The propositional object of a foundational attitude is false, but a foundational attitude is not a false belief. A false belief is intended to be an accurate representation, and the fact that it is false means that it is defective. It would better to replace it with its negation. In contrast, a foundational attitude is not intended to be an accurate representation, and it would be a loss to replace it with its negation, as I will show later in this chapter.

The alternative to denying that foundational attitudes are beliefs is arguing that beliefs do not have to "aim at truth."[2] But choosing that alternative would necessitate taking on too much opposing philosophy[3] and, hence, going on too great a detour. Worse, I doubt that I could convince the reader that it leads to the destination I desire. So I will not contest the claim that beliefs aim at truth.

There is ontological room for foundational attitudes in addition to beliefs. That beliefs necessarily aim at truth does not entail that all belief-like propositional attitudes do so as well. There could be some that have false content, that would therefore be defective if they were beliefs, but that are not beliefs. It cannot be shown a priori that all belief-like propositional attitudes must be beliefs. If it is true that beliefs aim at truth, it is conceptually true. But conceptual truths simply enable us to use words correctly: they do not enable us to determine what exists and what does not. Consequently, the supposed conceptual truth that beliefs aim at truth does not imply that there are no mental entities that are just like beliefs except that they do not aim at truth. I hypothesize that foundational attitudes are such mental entities. As for the appropriate verb to use in conjunction with them, I shall speak of *holding* foundational attitudes rather than believing them. I shall also speak of holding beliefs.

Since foundational attitudes are not beliefs and do not aim at truth, there is no reason why knowing that they are false should lead to their rejection. There is no counterpart to Moore's paradox here.[4] While it may be paradoxical to say "It is Tuesday but I do not believe that it is," a person can consciously and consistently affirm that he holds a foundational attitude but deny the truth of its propositional content. In this respect, a foundational attitude is like an assumption rather than a belief. We make assumptions for reasons other than that they are true. Indeed, sometimes we make them in order to show that their propositional content is false. Since foundational attitudes do not aim at truth, our being moral agents because of them will not prevent us from discovering the truth about human morality and discovering it will not result in our becoming amoral. For us to justifiably conclude that either outcome would occur, it would have to be the case that, like beliefs, foundational attitudes aim at truth.

The content of the foundational attitudes I require for my theory is a proposition expressed by a statement of the form, "*I am essentially of objective and independent intrinsic value throughout my existence*" – or, to use a convenient abbreviation, "*I am of value**." I use the starred term "value*" instead of the plain term "value" to indicate that I am using the term in a sense that I have defined stipulatively. As for the qualifiers, an entity is essentially valuable when it is valuable in every possible world in which it exists. It is objectively valuable when its value is not a function of anyone's desiring or valuing it. It is independently valuable when its value does not depend on any other property it possesses. And it is intrinsically valuable when it is not merely instrumentally valuable. If something is valuable*, then it is logically true that it is wrong to damage or destroy it and right to preserve it from damage or destruction, *ceteris paribus*.

Since foundational attitudes are biological adaptations, the referent of the first person pronoun in "I am of value*" is a biological organism, not a metaphysical entity such as a self or person that is distinct from the organism. I use the word, "person," merely as a synonym for "human organism" or "human organism with a foundational attitude." What is valuable* is the organism itself, not its life.[5] The contents of any two individuals' foundational attitudes express different propositions, but that is not important because the different propositions are expressed by indexed statements of the same form.

HOW FOUNDATIONAL ATTITUDES AFFECT ACTION

Foundational attitudes help counteract prudential weakness of the will, or *akrasia*. As I shall argue in the next chapter, this is the reason there was selection for them – counteracting prudential *akrasia* is their evolutionary function. What I mean by prudential weakness of the will is this: someone has at least two competing desires, he knows that satisfying one serves his interest to a greater extent than does satisfying the other, but nonetheless he acts so as to satisfy the latter rather than the former. It is *prudential* weakness of the will because only the interests of the agent are at stake; it contrasts with moral weakness of the will, which involves the interests of others. For instance, consider someone who knows that smoking is expensive and harmful but takes it up anyway because it is "cool." He desires money and health and he desires to appear "cool." Satisfying the former desire is more in his interest than satisfying the latter. Since he satisfies the latter rather than the former, however, he exhibits prudential weakness of the will.

I use the terms "*akrasia*" and "weakness of the will" because they are the traditional terms for this sort of phenomenon. However, I use them as stipulated and do not have an ontological commitment to the existence of something called a will that can be weaker or stronger. Like most modern English speakers, I speak of sunrise and sunset without thereby endorsing a geocentric view of the universe. My use of "weakness of the will" is analogous to my use of "sunrise." As the example of smoking shows, there is no reason to think that our strongest desire must be the one whose satisfaction would best serve our interests. I posit foundational attitudes to help explain why people do not exhibit prudential weakness of the will more often than they do.

Foundational attitudes can counteract prudential weakness of the will because they are related to behaviour in the same way that beliefs are, even though they do not aim at truth. False beliefs have the same effect on action as true beliefs; so do false foundational attitudes.

The relevant aspect of the relationship is this: if we act and if we do not act in ways whose true descriptions are consistent with both a proposition we hold and its negation, then we tend to act in ways whose true descriptions are consistent with the proposition we hold and inconsistent with its negation, that is, inconsistent with its contradictory and its contraries. The second conjunct in the antecedent is not a mistake. For example, any true desciption of my drinking coffee this morning would be consistent with "Socrates was the wisest man in Athens." The same description would also be consistent with "Socrates was not the wisest man in Athens." If a true description of my action were not consistent with both, then one combination or the other would entail a contradiction. But neither does. No one can act consistently with the *conjunction* of a proposition and its negation, but I do not contend that it is possible to do so. A true description of an action is consistent with both a proposition and its negation whenever they are irrelevant to the causal explanation of the action. Elliptically, we can say that we have dispositions not to act inconsistently with propositions that we hold or that we have disinclinations to act inconsistently with them.

A disinclination to act inconsistently with a proposition is not the same as a disposition to act consistently with it. The latter entails the existence of an inclination to act even in the absence of any desires to act. The former does not. Disinclinations are consistent with the motivational inertness of beliefs in the absence of desires. Dispositions to act are not.

The notion of acting consistently with a proposition can be explained as follows. A person acts consistently with a proposition if and only if the proposition is consistent with every otherwise complete and accurate description of his act that excludes every set of propositions that entails a proposition expressed by a statement of the form "A occurs in a world such that *p*," where "A" is the act and "*p*" is a proposition. The exclusion is necessary because if some description of the act entailed a description of the world in which it was performed, it would be possible to act consistently only with true propositions. A person acts inconsistently with a proposition if and only if the proposition is inconsistent with at least one such description of his act. There is no difficulty with the notion that a proposition can be inconsistent with a description of an act. A true description of an act is a set of propositions, and it is always possible to add another proposition so that the augmented set entails a contradiction.

Here is an example to illuminate the notion of acting consistently with a proposition. Suppose that someone wants to have a missed examination excused by providing a reason for his absence. Suppose that he believes that the only acceptable excuses are illness and bereavement. He will probably not act inconsistently with the proposition, "Illness and bereavement are the only acceptable excuses." Writing that he had watched the football final on television on the appropriate form would be acting inconsistently with the proposition. It would imply that it is not true that illness and bereavement are the only acceptable excuses. Therefore, he will probably not write it on the form even if it is true. He has a disinclination to do that and many other things. To put it another way, if someone wants to have a missed examination excused by providing a written excuse, believes that illness and bereavement are the only acceptable excuses, and writes that he spent the time watching football, then he is committed to a contradiction. The contradiction is that illness and bereavement are the only acceptable excuses and it is not the case that they are the only excuses.

The reason I think that we tend not to act inconsistently with propositions we believe is that we can often successfully predict what people will do when we are aware of their beliefs and desires (including the relative strengths of their desires). If believing a proposition did not mean that it was more probable that we would act consistently with it and inconsistently with its negation when we did not act consistently with both, knowing what people believe would not help us predict their actions, because the probability of their acting inconsistently with a proposition would be equal to, or greater than, the probability of their acting consistently with it.[6] But knowing the propositions people believe does help us to predict what they will do. So, if someone believes a proposition, it must be the case that he is inclined not to act inconsistently with it.

This claim does not commit me to philosophical behaviourism. Beliefs do not have to be dispositions to behave in certain ways in order for the foregoing to be true. For instance, people will have dispositions not to act inconsistently with propositions provided they have a disposition to maintain consistency between their beliefs and a tendency to believe truly about the nature of their actions. If one wished to maintain a consistent set of beliefs, if one tended to believe truly about the nature of one's acts, and if the descriptions of some acts entailed the negations of existing members of one's set of beliefs, one would have to avoid performing those acts. In other words, beliefs, a disposition to maintain consistency, and a propensity to believe truly about one's own actions, would produce dispositions not to act inconsistently with the beliefs. The beliefs need be nothing more than inert representations. Obviously, if existing beliefs were inert representations and were part of the causal explanation for the dispositions, the beliefs could not be the dispositions themselves.

We seem to believe truly about our actions far more often than not. Hence, it appears reasonable to believe that we have an inclination to believe truly about our acts. Inconsistency is relatively rare, almost never obvious, and unlikely to continue once it becomes obvious. Hence, it also appears that we have a disposition to maintain consistency between our beliefs.[7] I hypothesize that our disposition to maintain consistency is a disposition to maintain it between both our beliefs and our foundational attitudes. Consequently, the possessor of a foundational attitude has a disposition not to act inconsistently with a proposition expressed by a statement of the form "I am of value*."

We are now in a position to see how foundational attitudes can counteract prudential *akrasia*. When the possessor of a foundational attitude acts, he is more likely to act consistently with "I am of value*," and inconsistently with its negation when he does not act consistently with both. Hence, he will tend to preserve himself from damage or destruction, that is, to do things that are in his long-term interest and to refrain from doing things that are not. Sometimes a person has a desire to pursue a long-term project that is in his interest but also has desires for short-term gain or transitory pleasure that are not. Sometimes he will not be able to satisfy all the desires. In those circumstances, his foundational attitude will tend to prevent him from attempting to satisfy desires for short-term gain or transitory pleasure instead of satisfying his desire to pursue the long-term project – it will help prevent him from succumbing to prudential weakness of the will.

Because foundational attitudes reduce the probability of prudential weakness of the will, the result is an increased probability that their possessors will succeed at the long-term projects that they desire to complete. However, there is no guarantee that interfering desires will not overwhelm both the desire to complete the project and the influence of foundational attitudes. The fact that imprudent desires can be successfully countered by foundational attitudes often enough that there is selection for foundational attitudes does not mean that they can always be successfully countered. Foundational attitudes supplement desires to complete long-term projects and tip the balance more in their favour. They do not guarantee the outcome.

Of course, foundational attitudes do not interfere with the satisfaction of desires for pleasure or gain in the short term unless satisfying them would interfere with projects that are in the agent's long-term interest. They may help us keep from smoking but they do not necessarily get in the way of a swim on a hot summer's day. Satisfying short-term desires is consistent with holding that one is of value* when satisfying them does not adversely affect one's long-term interests. Evolutionary intuitionism is not a form of Puritanism.

A NATURAL MORAL COMMUNITY

Each individual with a foundational attitude cares about himself qua valuable* entity: he has a disposition not to act as though he was not of value*. People also have a disposition to acknowledge at least some others qua valuable* entities. The result of acknowledging another as being of value* is an extended foundational attitude. The content of an extended foundational attitude is a proposition expressed by a statement of the form "*I am of value* and* N^1 *is of value* to exactly the same extent as I am and … and* N^k *is of value* to exactly the same extent as I am*," where "N^n" is a name, pronoun, or definite description that refers to another person who possesses a foundational attitude (a possessor). A person who comes to care about at least one other individual possessor qua valuable* entity is committed to care about everyone with a foundational attitude, as I shall explain in a moment.

The move from some others to all others is a logical matter. In contrast, there is no logical route from caring about oneself to caring about others, contrary to the views of philosophers like Alan Gewirth.[8] A person could fail to adopt an extended foundational attitude but remain logically consistent; he could consistently hold that he, and he alone, was of value*. Someone with a foundational attitude has no problem holding that he is of value*. He has no choice: he has evolved to hold it. Since he does not hold that his value* supervenes on any of his non-moral properties, he could be a consistent moral solipsist. He immediately apprehends himself as being of value* but he does not immediately apprehend others as being of value and logic cannot compel him to do so. For now, I shall just assume that foundational attitudes are supplemented by a naturally selected disposition to acknowledge at least some other possessors as being equal in value*. I shall argue for the existence of the disposition in the next chapter.

While a person could consistently hold that he alone was of value*, the situation changes once he acknowledges another possessor as being of value*. Once he has done that, the lack of a relevant difference between the possessor he acknowledges and all other possessors commits him to acknowledge all other possessors as being of value*. To say that someone is committed to acknowledge all other possessors is not to say that since he has acknowledged one and since he has an obligation to be consistent, he must acknowledge all. Such a gloss presupposes pre-existing obligations, and I am now only in the process of explaining their origin. Rather, it is to say that it is not possible for the person to acknowledge one without acknowledging all – despite the fact that he can delude himself that it is possible. In other words, the act of acknowledging one cannot be separated from the act of acknowledging all. They are necessarily the very same act. The commitment to acknowledge all when one acknowledges one transforms the set of all actually existing possessors and potential possessors of foundational attitudes into a community.

Philosophers who hold that moral properties supervene on non-moral properties would expect the argument to be that some people have a non-moral property in virtue of which they are of value*, that others have the property as well, that it must be the case that the latter are valuable* if the former are, and that the former would be inconsistent if they held that they were of value* and did not also hold that the latter were of value*. This sort of argument is not available to evolutionary intuitionism because value* does not supervene on other properties. Value* is objective and independent and is not actually instantiated. It does not follow, however, that evolutionary intuitionism is out of luck.

We must distinguish the grounds for attributing value to someone or something from the grounds for judging someone to be consistent or not. Possessing the non-moral properties on which value supposedly supervenes justifies attributing value to the possessor of the non-moral properties. However, a person's commitment to attribute value to other possessors of the same non-moral properties is a function of the lack of a relevant difference. The fact that they possess the same non-moral properties means that there is no relevant difference, but it is the lack of a relevant difference that bears the weight of the commitment. Someone could be inconsistent in his attributions of value even if he were mistaken about the properties on which value supervenes.

If someone acknowledges another as being of value* and if the acknowledgment is not random, then the possessor whom he acknowledges will have what he takes to be symptoms of being of value*. He is committed to acknowledge as being of value* everyone who exhibits the same symptoms. A physician would be inconsistent if he diagnosed a patient with certain symptoms as having measles but diagnosed another patient with the same symptoms as suffering from another malady. This is true even if he is ignorant of the cause of the condition. Similarly, a sceptic can consistently hold that he is the only organism with a mind. He has access to his own mind in a way that he has access to no other. However, if he accepted that another organism had a mind, he would be inconsistent if he did not also accept that every other organism with the same symptoms of possessing a mind also had one. The possessor of a foundational attitude can be inconsistent in the same way even if, as in the case of the physician, he is ignorant of the causes. Therefore, someone who acknowledges some other possessors with the symptoms of being of value* is committed to acknowledge all other possessors who exhibit the same symptoms.

All mature possessors exhibit the symptoms. The symptoms are readily noticeable and, as I shall argue in the next chapter, there is selection for the ability to recognize them. The chief symptom is that someone acts as though he has an extended foundational attitude and therefore cares for at least some others as though they were valuable*.

Possessors are committed to hold that actually existing *potential* possessors are of value* just as actually existing actual possessors are. An actually existing potential possessor is an individual who does not have a foundational attitude but who will acquire one if the normal course of his development is not arrested, distorted, or ended prematurely. When Cain acknowledges that Abel is of value*, he acknowledges that Abel is of value throughout Abel's entire existence, because by definition, to hold that someone is of value* is to hold that he is of value throughout his existence. Moreover, otherwise, possessing value* would be contingent on possessing other, non-moral properties, and value* does not supervene on non-moral properties. In other words, Cain must hold that Abel would have been of value* even at times when Abel did not in fact hold that he was of value*. Abel's being of value* does not depend on his actually holding that he is of value* any more than it depends on any of his other properties. But if Cain is committed to hold that Abel was of value* when the latter was merely a potential possessor of a foundational attitude, he is committed to hold that all actually existing potential possessors are of value* also. If he has no grounds to justify denying that Abel was of value* when Abel did not actually hold that he was of value*, he has no grounds for denying that any other potential possessors are of value* either.

It is important, then, to know when possessors come into existence. When we ask when possessors of foundational attitudes come into existence, we are in effect asking when biological organisms come into existence. This is because a foundational attitude is a naturally selected adaptation and adaptations are features of biological organisms. Hence, the natural and obvious answer to our question is that a human possessor of a foundational attitude comes into existence with the completion of the process of conception. From the biological point of view, organisms like human beings are the same organism from zygote to dying oldster. They do not divide into daughter organisms, unless we count cases of identical twins, and they are not part of some larger organism. There is biological continuity in the stages leading from the zygote to the person with a foundational attitude, and there is no identifiable individual organism prior to fertilization. Hence, since they began as fertilized ova, possessors of foundational attitudes are committed to regard the fertilized ova out of which they developed as identical with themselves qua biological organisms. If the origin of the potential possessor occurred later than conception, value* would supervene on our non-moral properties, and that state of affairs is incompatible with evolutionary intuitionism. (Incidentally, the fact that fertilized ova are potential possessors does not lead to a blanket prohibition of abortion, as we shall see in chapter 4.)

The question of when a biological organism that is now an adult with a foundational attitude came into existence is obviously not the same as the question of when the organism became a person if personhood is defined as the possession of a certain range of mental properties and capacities. If it is so defined, organisms that are now adults with foundational attitudes will have come into existence well before they became persons. Fertilized ova do not possess any mental properties or capacities, so they do not have the mental properties and capacities that define personhood. Many potential possessors of foundational attitudes, and perhaps some actual possessors, are not persons in this sense.

Potential possessors obviously do not exhibit the symptoms of possessing a foundational attitude. If we are committed to acknowledge potential possessors as being of value*, we are also committed to acknowledge asymptomatic actual possessors – like infants – as well as mature possessors who do exhibit the symptoms. In sum, if there are foundational attitudes, then someone who acknowledges some other possessors is committed to acknowledge all other actual and potential possessors throughout their entire existence. However, the fact that he has that commitment does not entail that he explicitly or consciously acknowledges all of them, that he is inclined to do so, that he wants to do so, that he would want to do so if he were fully rational, or that it is in his interest to do so. The fact that someone is committed to hold that fetuses are of value* does not entail that everyone consciously holds that they are or that surveys of people's beliefs would be illuminating. It does not entail that there are no countervailing influences or even that there are no countervailing biological influences. There can be a gap between what someone actually does and what he is *committed* to do, a gap between what he actually does and what he *ought* to do. As we shall see, there are ways in which people can evade their commitments.

DESIRE-DEPENDENCE

If we now had a complete account of foundational attitudes and the moral community, the members of the community would sometimes have to sacrifice themselves, to die or suffer significant injury, in order to save a greater number of other members. It would be inconsistent to hold that people are of value* and not to take steps to preserve them from damage or destruction even if those steps had to involve the sacrifice of a smaller number for a larger. For instance, it would be necessary to cannibalize a healthy person for spare parts to use in surgical and medical procedures if more lives could be saved in that way. However, if evolutionary intuitionism is to give us a plausible account of human morality, it cannot have this implication. I hypothesize therefore that foundational attitudes have a particular contingency that I will call "desire-dependence." As in the case of the disposition to acknowledge some others as being of value*, the explanation for the existence of this feature is evolutionary and must wait until the next chapter. The primary form of desire-dependence is the state of affairs such that a person's extended foundational attitude depends on its being possible for him to desire to avoid significant injury at least as much as anything else when he acts, no matter what he might be trying to do. A community of individuals with desire-dependent extended foundational attitudes would more closely resemble the actual moral community than a community of individuals with non-contingent extended foundational attitudes would, because self-sacrifice would be obligatory in the latter community but supererogatory in the former.

To understand desire-dependence, it is necessary to distinguish the content of a foundational attitude qua proposition (full stop) from the content of a foundational attitude qua proposition that the holder would be inconsistent to deny (verbally or through action). While the former exists independently of what anyone holds (the state of someone's holding some proposition), the latter does not. Physical events cannot affect the former, but they can affect the latter by affecting the physical basis of the state of holding it. The former is an abstract entity. The latter is a physical entity analogous to an inscription. Desire-dependence is possible because it concerns the content of a foundational attitude qua proposition that the holder would be inconsistent to deny, and not the content of a foundational attitude qua proposition (full stop). It is possible because it is a matter of physical "inscriptions," not abstract propositions.

The desire-dependence of a foundational attitude is analogous to an arrangement in which there is an illuminated light bulb, the appropriate wiring, and a circuit breaker that cuts the flow of electricity to the bulb when it is tripped. The bulb, the wiring, and the breaker in the "on" position are analogous to the physical basis of the attitude. The illumination is analogous to the attitude itself. Desiring to do something more than to avoid significant injury is tripping the breaker, the result being that the light, the foundational attitude, "goes out." The foundational attitude "comes on" again when the desire weakens. The physical basis for the *possibility* of the foundational attitude is permanent – when the breaker is tripped, the light is extinguished, but the wiring is not ripped out. Saying that someone would be inconsistent if he did not sacrifice himself would be like saying that the light could stay on, and the illumination persist, after the breaker had been tripped.

To take another analogy, it would be like a situation in which one could not display a valid argument on a computer screen because the act of typing in the first part of the conclusion caused an essential premise to disappear from the screen. For instance, a computer might be programmed in such a way that ordinarily, the screen displayed the propositions, *p* and *(~p v (q & r))* but that the very act of typing in the first part of the proposition that follows logically, "*(q &*," would result in the disappearance of *p* from the screen. The two propositions initially displayed entail *(q & r)*, but it is nonetheless impossible to display all three on the screen. Metaphorically speaking, it is necessary to display the complete argument in order for someone to be committed to sacrifice himself. Self-sacrifice remains a voluntary option, however, because the desire-dependence of foundational attitudes does not preclude possessing a desire stronger than the desire to avoid significant injury. The point here is that there is no commitment to sacrifice oneself, not that it is impossible to do so or to desire to do so.

There are other forms of desire-dependence in addition to the primary form. An individual's extended foundational attitude is also conditional on his being able (when he acts) to desire to preserve his kin from significant injury and to do so more than anything else except to avoid significant injury to himself. If he desired an end that was incompatible with preserving his kin (other than avoiding significant injury to himself), if he desired it more than he desired to preserve his kin, and if he therefore attempted to satisfy it, his foundational attitude would vanish. While free to prefer kin to non-kin, someone would also be free to prefer his dependent offspring to his dependent parents: the asymmetry would increase fitness. A person's foundational attitude would also almost certainly depend on his being able (when he acts) to desire to preserve friends or those with whom he enjoys mutually beneficial relationships more than anything else except to preserve his kin and to avoid significant injury to himself. The three forms of desire-dependence form a hierarchy with the first form outranking the second and the second outranking the third.

Because of the last two forms of desire-dependence, possessors of foundational attitudes can have commitments to family and friends that they do not have to strangers, as we shall see. However, desire-dependence does not create commitments. Instead, it creates spheres within which someone is free from them with respect to some other people under certain conditions. Perhaps the best way to put it is that as a result of the desire-dependence of extended foundational attitudes, people sometimes have exemptions from commitments when it comes to strangers that they do not have with respect to family and friends. Possessors of extended foundational attitudes that were not contingent in this way would be committed to impartiality. Desire-dependence enables us to be partial under certain conditions.

Desire-dependence helps provide a plausible morality only if foundational attitudes are false. If they were true, desire-dependence could not free us from any commitments. Foundational attitudes can be desire-dependent but an objective fact that we were of value* could not. Moreover, we cannot get a plausible morality by assuming that someone's value* depends on his foundational attitude and that when his foundational attitude vanishes, so does his value*. Suppose value* depended on the property of having a foundational attitude and that one person with a foundational attitude was committed to sacrificing himself for two others. As long as he held his foundational attitude, he would be committed to sacrificing himself. There would be no escape if his foundational attitude vanished, however, because the others would still hold their foundational attitudes and would still be valuable* and because there is no objection to sacrificing the valueless* for the valuable*. If he could not bring himself to sacrifice himself, others would be free to sacrifice him. There does not appear to be any more complex property on which value* could be grounded with the consequence that he would not have to sacrifice himself. Moreover, the value* of one person could not depend on another's having a foundational attitude. Hence, there would be no way out of the difficulty if we really were of value*; false foundational attitudes are necessary for a plausible morality. As we shall see in chapter 6, however, the falsity of foundational attitudes does not entail that there are no moral facts or that there are no true moral beliefs.

THE TYPES OF MORAL FACTS

By hypothesis, the relations between desire-dependent extended foundational attitudes and acts (mediated by their true descriptions) constitute moral facts. The identification may appear arbitrary, but it is no more arbitrary than in the case of any other theoretical entities. Moreover, this kind of arbitrariness is inevitable in ethics. Many commentators cannot conceive of human morality lacking a *function*, but if our moral capacity is a by-product, it must be *functionless*, because as a by-product, it is not *for* anything in any sense whatsoever. It may bind us, but it does not serve us. Hence, one must initially assume either that morality has a function, as the adaptationist and most other ethicists do, or that it does not, as the intuitionist does. One cannot prove either the adaptationist or the intuitionist assumption a priori, of course, but only try to determine which sort of theory best accounts for, and accommodates, our moral experience. When adaptationist evolutionary ethicists and others identify certain beliefs and dispositions as *moral* beliefs and dispositions because they serve the hypothetical purpose of human morality, they are being just as arbitrary. Identifying as moral facts the relations between foundational attitudes and acts must be justified by their explanatory power, which will become apparent as we proceed.

It is necessary to consider both whether someone's actions are compatible with his desiring to preserve himself, his kin, and his friends at least as much as anything else, when he acts, and whether the acts are consistent with the content of his foundational attitude. Consequently, there are four basic types of moral facts. To avoid too much complex repetition, I have to introduce more terminology here. First, an act is *content-consistent* if and only if it is consistent with the content of an agent's foundational attitude. Otherwise, it is content-inconsistent. Second, an act is *desire-compatible* if and only if the agent can perform it while desiring to avoid significant injury to himself (at least as much as anything else), to preserve his kin (at least as much as anything else except to avoid significant injury to himself), etc., and to preserve his friends (at least as much as anything else except to avoid significant injury to himself and to preserve his kin). Otherwise, it is desire-incompatible.

The first of the four types of moral facts exists in connection with acts that are both desire-compatible and content-consistent. The evolutionary intuitionist hypothesis is that moral judgments that such acts are permissible would be true. If, in addition, a desire-compatible and content-consistent act were the only such act available to an agent, then it would be obligatory.

The second type of moral fact is connected with acts that are desire-compatible but content-inconsistent. The evolutionary intuitionist hypothesis is that moral judgments that all such acts are impermissible would be true. Everyone with a foundational attitude has an obligation not to perform such acts and would commit himself to an inconsistent position by performing one. Suppose that Cain has an extended foundational attitude and holds that "I am of value* and Abel is of value* to the same extent that I am." Now, suppose that Cain kills Abel because the latter has annoyed him. From Cain's point of view, Abel's being annoying is outweighed by the value* he is committed to attribute to Abel. By killing Abel, Cain commits himself to the proposition that Abel is not valuable* because killing him is inconsistent with his being of value*. Hence, if Cain kills Abel, he is committed to hold both that Abel was of value* and that Abel was not of value*. In addition, Cain's killing Abel is inconsistent with Cain's being of value*. If it were not wrong for Cain to kill someone who was valuable* to the same extent as Cain himself, then it would not be wrong for Cain to be killed. If it were not wrong for Cain to be killed, then it could not be the case that Cain is of value*. Hence, if Cain kills Abel, he commits himself to the position that he, Cain, is both of value* and not of value*. It would be both content-consistent and desire-compatible for Cain to refrain from killing Abel. Therefore, Cain is committed not to kill Abel. By hypothesis, he has an obligation not to kill him.

Third, there are the moral facts that exist in connection with acts that are content-consistent but desire-incompatible. Such acts are not obligatory but they may be positively good, just as a drought-breaking rain is good. If they are positively good, such acts are supererogatory: saving others at the cost of one's own life is admirable but not obligatory. Finally, there are the moral facts connected with those rare acts that would be content-inconsistent if they were desire-compatible but that are not desire-compatible. An example of such an act would be provided by a person who did not believe in an afterlife and who wanted revenge on another so much that he killed the latter's innocent children while knowing for certain that exacting revenge would cost his own life. We could categorize him as morally insane but not as a culpable wrongdoer, although we could conclude that what he had done was bad in the way that natural disasters are bad. If we can judge that those who perform acts of supererogation are good, we can conclude that what this sort of person does is bad.

Occasionally, as a matter of circumstances and psychological make-up rather than pure will, someone may have a desire that is stronger than his desire to avoid significant injury to himself, in which case his desire to avoid significant injury is naturally outweighed. In order to develop a stronger desire deliberately, a person would have to have a desire stronger than his desire to avoid injury and to attempt to satisfy it. But the desire-dependence of his extended foundational attitude means that he can have no obligation to develop such desires even if they are necessary to ensure that he acts in ways that would be content-consistent (if his foundational attitude remained in place). Similar arguments go through for the other desire possibilities on which his foundational attitude depends. Thus, there is no way to intentionally circumvent the limitations on obligations that result from the desire-dependence of foundational attitudes.

Evolutionary intuitionism is a naturalistic theory. But the contents of extended foundational attitudes include normative concepts. Someone's being of value* is a reason not to damage or destroy him and a reason to preserve him from damage or destruction. Consequently, the hypothesized moral facts include an ineliminable and irreducible normative element. Hence, this analysis of moral properties is unlike naturalistic reductions in which moral properties are replaced by properties such as the property of maximizing happiness. I reject claims like the utilitarian contention that the property of being right is identical with the property of maximizing happiness. It is not just that there seem to be cases in which doing the right thing does not maximize happiness but also that such naturalistic properties are not the right sort of properties.

There are some potential objections. First, it might be thought that it is a moral fact that we always have an obligation not to commit suicide, which would be counter-intuitive. We do not have such an obligation, however. A person's desire to avoid death is usually conditional, and the conditions on which it depends vary from person to person. It can be weaker under some conditions than it is under others. (Inquiring into the nature of the conditionalization process is unnecessary.) If enough of the conditions are not satisfied, the desire to avoid death vanishes. Once it has gone, we can easily desire something else and act in order to satisfy that desire, which eliminates our foundational attitudes (because they are desire-dependent). For instance, severe pain may undermine the conditions for someone's desiring to avoid death. The pain may be so great that he even desires to commit suicide in order to end it. If he attempts to satisfy this desire, he eliminates his foundational attitude.

Another potential objection is that the truth of moral judgments is subjective because of the desire-dependence of foundational attitudes. This is not the case. Desire-dependence partly determines what the moral facts are and therefore what our moral judgments should be, but this dependence is not the sort that would make them subjective. It does not mean that our desires to avoid injury, to preserve our kin, and to preserve our friends are singly or jointly sufficient to cause us to hold that we are of value*. It does not mean that they entail the contents of our foundational attitudes. It does not mean that they make our moral judgments true.

Third, some critics might reason as follows. A moral judgment that an act is obligatory is true because in virtue of holding that he is of value*, etc., an agent is committed to perform the act. It is true because value* ought to be promoted, and the act promotes value*. But, the critics may say, since there are other values, there is no reason to promote value* alone. If it is assumed that evolutionary intuitionism ought to be interpreted as saying that we should promote value*, it will appear that there could be other values that ought to be promoted as well. Then questions would certainly arise as to why value* is of overriding importance, why we should promote it rather than other values, what outweighs it, and so on. In fact, however, the relevant question is not whether an act promotes value* but whether an act is consistent with the content of the agent's extended foundational attitude and compatible with his being able to possess the relevant desires. What matter are not quanta of value but the relations between entities that hold themselves to be valuable*. It is a mistake to speak of "promoting" value*.

Finally, it might be objected that what I have called moral facts depend on an obligation to be rational, which subsumes an obligation to maintain consistency, and that I have justified neither. This objection has no merit. By hypothesis, moral facts are *constituted* by the relevant relationships between acts and foundational attitudes. The moral fact that it is obligatory to perform an act is *constituted* by the fact that the performance of any other act would be inconsistent with the agent's desire-dependent extended foundational attitude. For every act that has the property of being inconsistent with one's foundational attitude, there is an obligation not to perform it. There is no justification for denying that the moral facts postulated are brute moral facts. It is necessary to explain their origin. It is not necessary to justify their existence, and demanding such a justification begs the question.

As mentioned above, the normativity present in the moral facts derives from the content of foundational attitudes. The obligations hypothesized by evolutionary intuitionism do not depend upon, do not include, and do not need to be supplemented by an obligation to maintain consistency with one's foundational attitude. Indeed, at most, to say that one ought to avoid acting inconsistently with one's foundational attitude is like saying that one should do one's duty. It is a form of shorthand. There is not a duty to do one's duty in the same way that there is a duty to care for one's children, and the duty to care for one's children does not derive from a duty to do one's duty. Similarly, there is no obligation not to act inconsistently with one's foundational attitude. At most, speaking as though there were such an obligation is an elliptical way of claiming that wrongful acts involve acting inconsistently with one's foundational attitude.

REFLEXIVE RATIONALIZATION

The moral facts determine what we ought to do, but of course we do not always do what we ought to do. There is more than one possible explanation for this. However, it will be useful to discuss one of them immediately, the phenomenon of "reflexive rationalization."

Consider three facts. First, foundational attitudes are permanent and resilient. Evidence of their falsity does not lead to their rejection. As I shall argue in the next chapter, they exist for reasons that have nothing to do with representing the world accurately, for reasons that have nothing to do with their truth-value, and they are too advantageous to be vulnerable to being eliminated as readily as false beliefs.

Second, an agent's acting content-consistently can be incompatible with his pursuit of his own interests. The evolutionary function of foundational attitudes is preventing prudential weakness of the will. Morality is an evolutionary by-product of foundational attitudes. From the perspective of the individual organism *qua* organism subject to individual selection, doing the right thing is a cost and not a benefit. Acting consistently with his foundational attitude is always in the interest of the possessor when it prevents prudential *akrasia*. It is not always in his interest when doing so merely ensures that he acts morally appropriately. In fact, it will often be contrary to his interests.

Third, possessors of foundational attitudes have good reason to hold that their actions are content-consistent. If someone has a foundational attitude, then he has a disposition not to act inconsistently with "I am of value*." But if he does act inconsistently with that proposition, then he is committed to hold the proposition "I am not of value*." If he believes truly about his action, then he holds a proposition that entails "I am not of value*." If someone holds the proposition *p*, then he will act consistently with *p* and inconsistently with its negation, *~p*, when he does not act consistently with both. If someone holds the negation or anything that entails it, then he will act consistently with *~p* and inconsistently with *p* when he does not act consistently with both. It is impossible to act in a way that is both inconsistent with a proposition and inconsistent with its negation. (If you acted inconsistently with *p*, then by the same token you would act consistently with *~p*. So if you acted inconsistently with *~p* as well, you would act both consistently and inconsistently with *~p*, which is impossible.) So, holding both means that he can act only in ways that are consistent with both. This negates whatever advantage there may be to holding the beneficial member of the pair. Hence, holding that one's actions are content-inconsistent will deprive one of the advantage of holding a foundational attitude. Being committed to a contradiction will exact a high price when one of the conjuncts of the contradiction is "I am of value*."

It follows that people who hold permanent and resilient foundational attitudes will tend either both to act consistently with them and to believe truly about their actions or both to act inconsistently with them and to believe falsely about their actions. This is merely a tendency, because people may exhibit moral weakness of the will. In cases of moral *akrasia*, a person acts inconsistently with his foundational attitude (or moral beliefs) but believes truly that his actions are inconsistent with it (or them). With moral *akrasia*, the person believes truly that his action is wrong, whereas with reflexive rationalization, he believes falsely that it is not wrong – which means that moral *akrasia* is distinct from reflexive rationalization.

Although moral *akrasia* is possible, it is relatively rare. People will therefore tend to follow one or the other of the two courses mentioned. Since it will sometimes be in a person's interest to act content-inconsistently, he will tend to believe falsely about the nature of his actions on those occasions. An ideal observer would see the agent as acting inconsistently (because he would know the true nature of the agent's act) but the agent will see himself as acting consistently (because he has deluded himself about the nature of his act).

People do engage in reflexive rationalization, or so I shall argue in later chapters. People do tend to believe falsely about the nature of their actions when they perform actions that are in their interest but that they hold, or are committed to hold, to be wrong. Reflexive rationalization is not the same sort of rationalization that people consciously devise in order to escape disapprobation. It is unconsciously devised solely to permit the rationalizer to maintain consistency between his propositional attitudes despite acting wrongly.

Reflexive rationalization enables moral agents to pursue their interests in immoral ways. It is an evolutionary attempt to obviate the influence of an evolutionary by-product that exists not because it is itself advantageous but because it is linked to an advantageous adaptation. There is selection for the ability to rationalize reflexively, but selection for a feature does not always lead to the development of an adaptation, because there can be simultaneous selection for its elimination as well. The balance in this case gives us evolutionary reasons to think that reflexive rationalization will remain relatively rare indefinitely, as I will argue in chapter 5. Since it will be relatively rare, an agent will still have a tendency not to act inconsistently with his foundational attitude. When reflexive rationalization occurs, what gives way is not a person's foundational attitude or his disposition to maintain consistency but his disposition to believe truly about his actions.

Because of desire-dependence people are not committed to do things that they would be committed to do if their foundational attitudes were not contingent in that particular way. Because of desire-dependence, they are not inconsistent when otherwise they would be. In contrast, someone who rationalizes reflexively maintains the consistency of the propositional attitudes in his mental storehouse while simultaneously failing to maintain the consistency between his propositional attitudes and his acts. According to evolutionary intuitionism, to act in ways that are inconsistent with one's desire-dependent extended foundational attitude is to act in ways that are wrong. People who rationalize reflexively do not become free of their moral obligations: they merely think that they do not have obligations that they do in fact have. Desire-dependence is a determinant of our obligations. Reflexive rationalization is just a means of evading them. The obligations still exist and reflexive rationalization is always wrong.

CONCLUSION

The theoretical apparatus of evolutionary intuitionism has now been fully displayed. I have introduced desire-dependent extended foundational attitudes as theoretical entities and have shown how their possessors come to form a natural moral community once they have acknowledged at least one other as being of value* as well. I have enumerated the types of moral facts qua relations between acts and foundational attitudes. I will demonstrate the power of this theoretical apparatus later on but my immediate aim is to provide an evolutionary account of the origin of foundational attitudes and to present some evidence for the truth of the evolutionary story.

3

The Evolution of Intuitionistic Organisms

INTRODUCTION

When a new adaptation comes into existence, the relations between an organism and its environment change. The organism has new capacities and, perhaps, new vulnerabilities. Given the requisite variation, the new adaptation can be supplemented by yet more adaptations that further increase the fitness of the organism or by compensating adaptations that reduce the vulnerabilities connected with it. There was, I believe, an evolutionary dialectic leading through a number of transitional forms to moral agents with moral intuitions. I am going to describe a course the dialectic might have taken. The account is not a "just-so" story, however. It enables us to make empirical predictions that are confirmed by observation. Evolutionary intuitionism is not entirely speculative.

EVOLUTIONARY INTUITIONISM AND ADAPTATIONIST EVOLUTIONARY ETHICS

As I have already pointed out, what we commonly call "evolutionary ethics" is *adaptationist*. But as I have also pointed out, evolutionary intuitionism is not adaptationist. It appeals to individual selection rather than kin selection, group selection, or reciprocal altruism. Whereas adaptationist evolutionary ethics says that morality is adaptive, evolutionary intuitionism denies that it is and claims instead that morality is a by-product. Once there are human beings with desire-dependent extended foundational attitudes, there are automatically moral facts and moral agents with moral intuitions as well. But an adaptation is a feature of an organism that exists because it causes increased viability or fertility in an organism, and morality has no role to play in the causal account of the development of desire-dependent extended foundational attitudes. Desire-dependent extended foundational attitudes increase the fitness of human beings, but they do not do so because they make them moral agents.

Adaptationist evolutionary ethics assumes that there is continuity between human beings and other species along a social/moral axis. Darwin thought so, writing that "any animal whatever, endowed with well-marked social instincts, the parental and filial affections being here included, would inevitably acquire a moral sense or conscience, as soon as its intellectual powers had become as well, or nearly as well developed, as in man."[1] Not all theorists hold that the intellectual powers have to be so advanced. Michael Stingl argues that chimpanzees can have true moral beliefs.[2] He points out that they share food except under conditions of abundance and scarcity and that the dominant male will punish youngsters who take too much but that older females will intervene if the punishment seems excessive. If the behaviour does not consist merely of instinctive responses to stimuli and if the goal is to maintain social cohesion, it seems to be true that chimpanzees should share food, that no individual should take more than his fair share, and that the punishment of cheaters should not be too harsh. Moreover, it appears reasonable to say that the chimpanzees can be said to know this.

What I disagree with is Stingl's identification of the fact that chimpanzees should share as a moral fact and his identification of the knowledge that they should as moral knowledge. If Stingl were really talking about moral facts and moral beliefs here, morality would be instrumental; it would have a function. But as mentioned in the previous chapter, the adaptationist and the intuitionist hypotheses about what is to be identified as the moral are on an equal footing at the outset. Neither the adaptationist nor the intuitionist is able to prove a priori that what he identifies as the moral really is the moral. They rely equally on theoretical entities. It would therefore beg the question to assume that morality is instrumental; it would be equally question-begging to assume that it is not. The dispute can be resolved only by determining whether instrumentalist or non-instrumentalist theories are better at accommodating and accounting for human moral experience.

I believe that instrumentalist theories like adaptationist evolutionary ethics fail to account adequately for what we observe. As I argued in chapter 1, adaptationist evolutionary ethics cannot explain the fact that some people believe that it is extraordinarily virtuous for a person to knowingly and secretly help people who are not his kin, who are not members of the same group, and with whom he does not have a relationship involving reciprocal altruism. Kin selection, group selection, and reciprocal altruism would all tend to eliminate both the benefactor and the people who approve of him. Moreover, the help is not the result of what I have called a misfire, because it is done knowingly. It is not self-advertisement, because it is done secretly. And it is not approved because approval is a tactic to persuade the gullible to be more altruistic than they otherwise would be – people who approve are also more likely to be more generous than others. In contrast, as we shall see in chapter 5, evolutionary intuitionism has no trouble explaining the phenomenon.

Adaptationism sees morality as an elaboration and development of the social. With evolutionary intuitionism, on the other hand, the social and the moral are discontinuous. According to evolutionary intuitionism, and contrary to Darwin, it is not inevitable that social animals become moral animals no matter to what extent their intellectual abilities increase. Foundational attitudes are an independent development that had nothing to do with our being social. We were already social animals when we acquired them, and initially, they probably made us less social. The social did not become the moral. Instead, in societies of possessors of foundational attitudes, the old social relations became governed by new considerations, by moral considerations. Some aspects of the old social relations were endorsed; others were condemned; and yet others ignored.

SELECTION FOR FOUNDATIONAL ATTITUDES

Foundational attitudes were naturally selected because they help combat prudential weakness of the will by improving an existing ability of human beings to plan, carry out, and preserve the fruits of projects that are in their long-term interests. They do so by counteracting the influence of desires whose satisfaction, or attempted satisfaction, would interfere with the successful completion of these projects. The adaptation is not insignificant, because it improved an existing ability rather than bringing it into existence – people could travel overland from one end of Canada to the other before the Canadian Pacific Railway was built but the existence of the CPR dramatically increased the probability both that people would start the journey and that they would complete it. One cannot determine the precise degree to which foundational attitudes improve our ability to carry out long-term projects, but it is probably substantial. Even a slight improvement would result in foundational attitudes spreading throughout the human population over time.

The case for foundational attitudes does not depend on there being no other possible explanation for our ability to carry out long-term projects or on there being no other contributing factors. I am not making a logical point but an empirical one. As long as our ability is imperfect, foundational attitudes will make us less prone to prudential weakness of the will no matter what else contributes to our ability. Foundational attitudes can form part of the explanation for our ability to carry out long-term projects as well as we do. The evidence that they do will be some of the empirical evidence presented later.

As long as we do not have a perfect ability to carry out long-term projects, there will be selection for anything that improves our ability. Our ability to pursue our long-term interests is certainly imperfect. The ability does not derive straightforwardly from a desire to survive. Members of many other species have a desire to survive but lack a capacity for long-term planning. The only behaviour among non-human animals that might be taken to indicate such a capacity is the caching of food by the members of some species.[3] Adding foresight is not enough to perfect the ability. Someone could foresee that attempting to satisfy a desire would be fatal to a long-term project that is in his interest but nevertheless not suppress the interfering desire: to foresee is not necessarily to care sufficiently about one's long-term interests. Even caring about one's future would not necessarily make the desire to complete the project stronger than the interfering desire. There are always students who party instead of studying, even though they know that they thereby put their future at risk. They may care, but they do not care enough. Therefore, there would be selection for foundational attitudes once they came into existence. People who possessed them would be biologically fitter than people who did not, because the attitudes would lead them to care more about what they foresaw when their long-term interests were at stake, which in turn would increase the probability that they would successfully complete long-term projects that were in their interest.

Given the requisite variation, there would have been selection for foundational attitudes that were resilient in the face of counter-evidence. There are no drawbacks to foundational attitudes that are robust enough to survive in any evidential environment; indeed, there are few, if any, environments in which an improved capacity to act in one's long-term interest would not increase fitness. This is especially true because foundational attitudes would not require anyone to work on long-term projects when doing so was not in his interest and because they would not interfere with the satisfaction of short-term desires unless the interference was beneficial. If we lacked evidentially resilient foundational attitudes, we would be in danger of losing them in circumstances in which possessing them was to our advantage. There is plenty to tell us that we are not of value*. The non-human world pays no heed to the value* we impute to ourselves, and other people may tell us that we are worthless. If they are more powerful and can get away with it, many other possessors of foundational attitudes will treat us as being worthless or as being only of instrumental value and reflexively rationalize their actions. Their actions are also evidence for our worthlessness. Hence, from the perspective of the organism, there are reasons why resilience is desirable and none why it is not.

There is what can be construed as empirical evidence that our foundational attitudes are resilient in the face of contrary evidence. People who are taught that they are worthless frequently suffer mental anguish. The existence of foundational attitudes would explain this anguish because if a person held that he was of value* and had the sense that others ought to regard him as valuable*, being told that he was worthless would have a negative impact. Moreover, those in this unfortunate situation do not end their mental suffering by accepting that they are worthless and saying, So what? Their failure to do so indicates that the source of their sense that others ought to regard them as valuable is resilient. If that source is their foundational attitudes, those attitudes survive in evidential environments that are extremely hostile. People may say that they are worthless, but this is a case in which actions – and reactions – speak louder than words.

For the same reasons that resilient foundational attitudes are a good thing, permanent ones are also desirable. Hence, in addition to selection for resilience, there would be selection for permanence. It would be disadvantageous to be in danger of losing a foundational attitude or to be able to rid oneself of it.

SELECTION FOR THE CONTENT OF FOUNDATIONAL ATTITUDES

Once we see that foundational attitudes could perform the function hypothesized for them, we have to ask why there was selection for them and not for propositional attitudes with a different content. The reason is that the proposition "I am essentially of objective and independent intrinsic value throughout my existence" is the simplest one that can be the object of a propositional attitude that improves the ability of people to plan, carry out, and preserve the fruits of projects that are in their long-term interest. The multiple modifiers do not make the proposition complex. Instead, they exclude complexity. To say that someone holds that he is of value* is to say that he holds that he is of value (full stop). If someone held that he was of value but did not hold that he was essentially of independent and objective intrinsic value throughout his existence, then he would hold both that he was of value and that he had some other property in virtue of which he was of value, and the former would depend on the latter. In other words, he would hold two propositions – "I am of value" and "I possess characteristic C" – and the first one would be contingent on the second. Of course, moral theorizing could result in someone with a foundational attitude acquiring a belief that there was a reason why he was of value. But acquiring the belief would not make his foundational attitude dependent on it.

Let us compare bare foundational attitudes and a "package" consisting of a belief in one's value and a reason for the value on which the belief depends. Once foundational attitudes had evolved, there would be no selection for a belief that set out a justification on which the foundational attitude depended unless the belief and the dependence relation served some other purpose. A "package" would be no better than a bare foundational attitude with respect to improving someone's ability to pursue long-term projects. Second, there is a higher probability that random mutation would produce foundational attitudes first, because they are less complex than a "package." The probability that a foundational attitude would be thrown up by chance is much greater than the probability that chance would throw up a foundational attitude plus a belief giving a reason for one's value plus a relationship of dependence between the two.

Third, if a "package" did arise, there would admittedly be selection for it (because it would improve its possessor's ability to carry out projects that are in his long-term interest), but there would be selective pressure for its elimination as well. With such a "package," someone would be more capable of acting in his own long-term interest, but he would also be required to sacrifice himself for others in order to maintain consistency. His "reason" for attributing value to himself would almost certainly be a "reason" to attribute value to others. If only a very small minority possessed the "package," as would undoubtedly be the case early on, its costs would almost certainly outweigh its benefits and the individuals possessing it would be quickly eliminated by natural selection. On the other hand, someone with the foundational attitude I postulate would have an advantage even if no one else possessed one. In a mixed population of people with bare foundational attitudes, people with "packages," and people with neither, people with bare foundational attitudes would inevitably soon predominate, because they would gain an advantage by exploiting people with "packages" in some circumstances.

If group selection were operating, "packages," rather than foundational attitudes, might evolve. In that case, much of what I am setting out here might very well remain the same. Meta-ethically, the overall picture would be more traditional, because it is now orthodox to think that value is a supervenient property. Of course, if group selection produced "packages," different groups might have different justifying beliefs, and there could be selection for innovations in the justifying belief if it were advantageous for one group to differentiate itself from others. It is doubtful that there would be a *universal* human morality, one that existed in all cultures, unless the relevant "package" held that we are of value and that our value supervenes on properties that are *essential* to our being human. If there were a universal human morality, it would be radically contingent unless it supervened on essential properties. The problem with this from the biological point of view is that species do not have essences.[4] Possessors of foundational attitudes hold that they are essentially of value, but actually they are not.

At any rate, there may be potential theoretical competitors for foundational attitudes as I have defined them. Hence, there may potentially be a family of theories like evolutionary intuitionism. However, I am not going to propose a competitor for foundational attitudes: I have none to propose and no inclination to try to solve the problems that a competitor would confront. I shall continue to assume that there are foundational attitudes as I have described them rather than "packages." The fact that it is possible that foundational attitudes have potential competitors in their own family does not entail that they are out of the running.

Not all propositions about being of value would improve someone's ability to act in his long-term interest if he held them. Two that would not are "I am of value because I am valued by a valuer that exists in an infinite hierarchy of valuers" and "I am of value because I am valued by a valuable* valuer." They would not improve a person's ability to act in his long-term interest because he, the valued, need not share the attitude of the valuer(s) toward him. The only value that would improve the ability of agents to act in their own long-term interest would be one that resulted from the reflexive valuing of the self. The valuing of oneself by others and one's own recognition of that valuing do not necessitate any reflexive valuing of the self. A person can consistently fail to value himself even when others value him and he knows that they do.

The proposition that someone's life is of instrumental value to him would do nothing to counter desires whose attempted satisfaction was not in his long-term interests. A person needs his life in order to satisfy desires that are not in his long-term interest just as much as he needs it in other cases. His recognition of this fact would at most lead to his having a second-order desire to preserve his life so that he could satisfy his first-order desires. There is no reason to think that it would have any effect on the first-order desires themselves. It need not result in his acquiring new ones, in old ones being eliminated, or in changes in the comparative strengths of his present desires. In short, holding that one's life is of instrumental value to oneself is consistent with acting in ways that are not in one's long-term interest and does nothing to improve one's ability to act in one's long-term interest. It does not follow that someone who holds that he is of value* holds that his life is not of instrumental value. The point here is that the proposition that our lives are of instrumental value will not improve our ability to carry out projects that are in our long-term interests.

SELECTION FOR EXTENDED FOUNDATIONAL ATTITUDES

Evolutionary intuitionism postulates a disposition to acknowledge at least some other possessors as being of equal value*. As mentioned in chapter 2, it is necessary to posit the disposition because a person could fail to adopt an extended foundational attitude but remain logically consistent; he could consistently hold that he, and he alone, was of value*. In order for it to be logically inconsistent for a person not to hold that others were of value*, foundational attitudes would have to be part of the sort of "package" that was rejected in the preceding section.

Foundational attitudes originated among human beings when they were already social animals living in small-scale societies. I believe that rules and norms like the ones that Stingl attributes to chimpanzees, albeit probably more complex and sophisticated, governed the interactions of members of these small-scale societies.[5] As mentioned in a previous section, foundational attitudes did not cause us to become social, co-operative organisms. Instead, they transformed social co-operation by giving their possessors an evolutionary advantage over non-possessors. Possessors could act more effectively in their long-term interests. As more and more individuals with foundational attitudes came into existence, opportunities to amplify the advantage through co-operation came about. Hence, there was selection for possessors of foundational attitudes who were capable of taking advantage of the opportunities.

First, there would have been selection for the ability of possessors to identify other possessors by recognizing the symptoms of a foundational attitude, because other possessors would be the only ones with whom possessors could profitably co-operate on advantageous long-term projects. Non-possessors would not be reliable on such projects. No matter how reliable people might be on short-term projects, such as gathering wood for a fire, they would not be as much help on long-term projects, such as gathering firewood for use the next winter. If a possessor co-operated with them, he would gain no advantage from having a foundational attitude, because either he would not achieve any long-term goals or he would expend unnecessary effort in achieving them. In the latter case, he would benefit others at a significant cost to himself. Consequently, possessors in a population of non-possessors would probably have been less social and less co-operative than non-possessors, because co-operation with non-possessors would have been unprofitable or costly. Co-operative relationships would have been re-established fully only with other possessors of foundational attitudes and within new social groups, groups reorganized in the light of the moral element introduced by extended foundational attitudes.

Second, there would have been selection for a disposition to acknowledge other possessors of foundational attitudes as being of value*. The mere ability to recognize other possessors would not have led to co-operation on long-term projects. The chief concern of prospective partners, who would have had to agree to participate in the projects, would be to avoid being exploited. Those least likely to exploit them would be those who regarded them as valuable* and who, therefore, had a concern for them for their own sake. People who could identify possessors of foundational attitudes but who failed to acknowledge them as being of value* would have failed to demonstrate to them that they would be reliable partners who would not exploit them. They would therefore have found it difficult to get others to agree to co-operate with them on long-term projects.

The attitude that others were of value* brought into existence a disposition to act consistently with the proposition that they were of value*, and inconsistently with its negation, in cases in which the organism did not act consistently with both. A person whose behaviour presupposed that others were of value* showed the others that he was reliable and not exploitative. Since there was typically a succession of long-term co-operative projects, sincerely acknowledging another as being of value* was obviously better than merely paying lip service to his putative value*, because the temptation to "defect" in any particular case was less. Imagine that someone held that he was of value* himself and that he had the capacity to act as though others were of value*, but that he did not in fact hold that they were. He would co-operate with them but he would always have it in the back of his mind that it might be profitable to "defect." If he did "defect," he would run the risk of doing so at the wrong time. In small-scale societies, it might never be opportune to do so. While pretending to care might lead to the same gains as actually caring, the costs might be higher, because someone who merely pretends that others are of value* has to fear that others are just pretending also and cannot really trust them. To the extent that he could, he would have to substitute surveillance and threats for trust. It would be better for him if the others really held that he was of value*, but people with extended foundational attitudes would do better to co-operate with one another than to co-operate with him. Hence, there would have been selection for possessors of foundational attitudes really holding that others are of value*.

Third, given the requisite variation, there would have been selection for a disposition to regard others as equally valuable*. Possessors both interacted with others who wanted to be treated at least as equals and were observed interacting with them. If they had been observed favouring themselves over the other participants in co-operative projects, they would have been revealed as undesirable partners. In the instances in which the observers were not also participants, the observers would have been able to inform on them. People with a disposition to regard others as being equally valuable* were less inclined to cheat and could form longer-lasting co-operative partnerships. The attitude "N is of value*" became "N is of value* to the same extent as I am." For obvious reasons, it would generally be disadvantageous for an individual to go further and hold "N is of value* to a greater extent than I am." Hence, "N is of value* to the same extent as I am" became "N is of value* to exactly the same extent as I am."

There would have been selection for a relation of dependence such that someone who lacked or lost a foundational attitude would lack or lose the attitude that others are of value*. In other words, there would have been selection for an arrangement in which no one held that others were of value* unless he held himself to be of value*. Any other arrangement would have had biological disadvantages but no advantages. For the same reason, there would have been no selection for a tendency to hold that non-possessors were of value*. A disposition to acknowledge non-possessors would have resulted in decreased biological fitness without any compensating advantages.

Finally, there was selection for the ability to recognize other possessors who acknowledged yet other possessors as being of value*, that is, to recognize not only the symptoms of a foundational attitude but also the symptoms of an extended foundational attitude.

Individuals with extended foundational attitudes would develop the capacity to recognize other individuals who possessed not merely foundational attitudes but extended foundational attitudes and who therefore would co-operate with them and not exploit them.

There was selection for the extended foundational attitude that produced the behaviour, not the behaviour itself. One could have the behaviour without the attitude but not the attitude without the behaviour (unless reflexive rationalization or weakness of the will was involved). Being moral must not be confused with appearing to be moral. Being moral is not instrumental; merely appearing to be moral would be. Indeed, people who make too ostentatious a display of their own virtue, rectitude, or charity are suspect for the very reason that they seem to be too concerned with appearances. If there had been possessors and those who merely acted as though they were possessors, there would have been selection for an ability to distinguish the latter from genuine possessors. It is possible to make the distinction. Helping others when there is no prospect of gain is one of the clearest signs that someone is a reliable co-operator, because it is one of the clearest signs that a person actually has a foundational attitude. The symptoms of being the possessor of an extended foundational attitude are readily discernible by possessors of foundational attitudes. Later, however, we will see that people can delude themselves about the moral status of others.

The fact that acting morally became a prerequisite for co-operation does not entail that morality is itself instrumental. Acting morally is a cost we incur in order to gain the advantages of co-operation; it is the price paid to secure the co-operation of others in long-term projects. The price must be paid precisely because morality is a by-product. It is the co-operation that has instrumental value. Morality acts as a signal, but it is not the case that there was selection for it because it acted as a signal. It is like other natural signs. It is a reliable indicator of a state of affairs, but it is not intended or designed to be a reliable indicator of that state of affairs. Nor does it persist because it is a reliable indicator. Acting morally is analogous to the spots that are a symptom of measles and that enable us to diagnose the condition. It is not the case that there was selection for spots because they enabled us to diagnose measles; they are a natural sign of the disease. It is not the case that they have a function and that their function is to enable us to diagnose measles even though they enable us to do so. On the contrary, they have no function at all. Similarly, acting morally is a natural sign that the agent has a foundational attitude. It does not follow that it has a function. The spots have no purpose; neither does being moral. Being moral is simply the chief symptom of the possession of a foundational attitude.

In the end, there were social and co-operative beings who were capable of interacting within a moral framework and who were linked by logical bonds. It might be thought that we could get to this stage in a single step through the development of extended foundational attitudes, that we were not social, co-operative, or moral before the development of foundational attitudes but that we acquired the three characteristics simultaneously with their development. But the notion is implausible. First, other primates are social and co-operative but do not appear to have foundational attitudes, since they do not have projects that they work on with a view to their own long-term welfare. If other primates are social and co-operative although they do not have foundational attitudes, there seems to be no reason why human beings could not be social and co-operative without possessing them. Second, the idea of a single step implies that a complex feature developed all at once instead of through a series of simple features. It would be improbable for the same reasons that the "packages" discussed in the previous section were improbable. The incremental development of a complex whole, each stage being a small improvement on the previous stage, is more probable than the complex's developing fully formed all at once.

The increased fitness of human beings with extended foundational attitudes probably ensured that they rapidly increased as a proportion of the population. They would all have been disposed to acknowledge others as valuable* and to develop co-operative relationships with them. What Richard Dawkins calls "the Green Beard Altruism Effect"[6] could have occurred. If organisms with green beards help only other organisms with green beards, then organisms with green beards should increase particularly quickly within a population. Similarly, for organisms with foundational attitudes: the proportion of such organisms could have increased particularly quickly. In the end, whether the green beard altruism effect occurred or not, there were no subgroups of human beings, all of whose members, or even a much larger than average proportion of whose members, lacked them.

SELECTION FOR DESIRE-DEPENDENCE

As we have seen, foundational attitudes give a person an advantage in carrying out long-term projects that are in his own interest, and extended foundational attitudes give him an advantage by transforming him into a potential beneficiary of long-term co-operation with others. But if this were the whole story, the gains from long-term co-operation would potentially be offset by terrific fitness costs. People with extended foundational attitudes would be vulnerable because acting consistently with the attitude that the members of a group of entities are valuable* requires minimizing damage to, or destruction of, them. In some cases, in order to meet this requirement an agent would have to sacrifice himself. The potential fitness gains achievable through long-term co-operation could very well not be worth it if an agent had to die or be badly injured for the sake of others. Extended foundational attitudes could be biologically disastrous for many of their possessors.

People could not simply act inconsistently with "I am of value*" on those occasions on which acting consistently with it would require self-sacrifice, because in that case their foundational attitudes and their beliefs about their actions (because they tend to hold truly about their actions) would entail a contradiction. As indicated in chapter 2, this inconsistency would have high costs as well. If someone holds a proposition, then it is far more probable that he will act consistently with it and inconsistently with its negation when he does not act consistently with both. If he holds both a proposition and its negation, he will not be able to act in ways that are inconsistent with either. All his acts will have to be consistent with both. But the whole advantage of a foundational attitude depends on its making it more probable that he will act inconsistently with its negation when he does not act consistently with both. Hence, the benefits of having a foundational attitude are negated when its possessor acts inconsistently with it and, as a result, holds something that entails its negation as well. The problem might vanish of its own accord over time as the agent gradually forgot, but it would still be a problem.

One could maintain consistency by rationalizing reflexively and falsifying the descriptions of one's acts in one's own mind. But, as I shall point out in chapter 5, doing so is not always possible or desirable for various reasons and especially because potential partners in long-term co-operation would tend to reject such rationalizers.

Consequently, reflexive rationalization would be an imperfect solution. It would not enable people to avoid self-sacrifice causing significant injury on all occasions and might result in their losing the benefits of long-term co-operation even if it did. Reflexive rationalization would work on some occasions, but not all occasions on which it could be used would be propitious.

Desire-dependence, which was discussed in the previous chapter, does provide a satisfactory solution. It is not possible for someone who knowingly sacrifices himself to desire to avoid significant injury at least as much as anything else when he sacrifices himself. If someone had a commitment to sacrifice himself, then, when he attempted to fulfil his commitment, it would have to be the case both that it was possible for him to desire to avoid significant injury at least as much as anything else and that it was not. That state of affairs would be impossible. Hence, if an agent's extended foundational attitude was desire-dependent, he would not have a commitment to sacrifice himself; refusing to sacrifice himself in order to minimize the loss of what he is committed to take to be of value* would be consistent with his holding that he is of value*. Failing to sacrifice oneself would be inconsistent if one's extended foundational attitude were independent and one could keep on holding it while one sacrificed oneself; it would not be inconsistent if the extended foundational attitude was desire-dependent. The desire to survive uninjured, which is ordinarily supplemented by the attitude, would override the foundational attitude in those instances in which they conflicted.

The first form of desire-dependence would be a product of individual selection. The second form would be a product of kin selection. It would free someone to prefer kin to non-kin. Further, as mentioned in chapter 2, someone would also be free to prefer his dependent offspring to his dependent parents, because his children can contribute more to his genetic legacy than his parents can. Grandparents would have the same bias. The third form of desire-dependence would be a product of reciprocal altruism that would enable a person to favour his friends over strangers in cases in which he was unable to preserve both friends and strangers.

The three forms of desire-dependence would be related hierarchically, the desire to avoid injury to oneself taking precedence over the desire to preserve kin, which in turn would take precedence over the desire to preserve friends. In other words, a person would be free to prefer kin to friends, and free to prefer himself to both kin and friends in cases in which he could not preserve all. Any other arrangement would be less advantageous. Suppose, for instance, that a person's desire to preserve himself did not take precedence over his desire to save his kin. That arrangement could result in a catastrophic loss of fitness before a person could actualize his reproductive potential. Sacrificing oneself for a child when one would be likely to have more later on would not be the way to maximize one's genetic legacy. Being committed to do so would decrease fitness. Moreover, if a person saved his child at the cost of his own life, he might decrease the child's own long-term viability and put his other offspring at risk as well. In short, if a person's desire to preserve himself were consistently outranked by his desire to preserve his offspring, he would be deprived of the opportunity to judge whether his sacrifice would be worthwhile and to act accordingly. Self-sacrifice remains an option, however. Although no one is obligated to sacrifice himself for the sake of his offspring, he can have a strong desire to preserve them and even be willing to give his life for them.

EMPIRICAL EVIDENCE

If there are foundational attitudes and if they are part of the foundation of human morality, we can make at least three major empirical predictions. First, every human society will have a moral code. Second, people will rationalize reflexively. And third there will be a correlation between being a rationalizing moral agent and being able to carry out long-term projects as successfully as human beings normally do.

According to the first prediction, morality will be universal: there will be no human society or culture that does not include moral agents who make moral judgments and who appear to be influenced by the judgments they make. Given evolutionary intuitionism, the reasons for this are as follows. As already argued, possessors of foundational attitudes were fitter than non-possessors and became a larger and larger proportion of the human population. Possessors of extended foundational attitudes were similarly fitter than possessors of unextended foundational attitudes and increased in a like manner. Possessors of contingent foundational attitudes were fitter than were people whose extended foundational attitudes were not contingent. They also increased as a proportion of the total population. Although morality will be universal, there can also be variation in moral codes, for reasons that I will discuss in chapter 5.

According to the second prediction, people will sometimes rationalize reflexively, because acting consistently with one's foundational attitude can be disadvantageous in certain circumstances. Similarly, acting inconsistently with it and believing truly about one's actions will also be disadvantageous, because it deprives the agent of the benefits of his foundational attitude by committing him to a contradiction. Being committed to a contradiction, he can act only in ways that are consistent with both his foundational attitude and its negation. The alternative is to maintain consistency by believing falsely about the nature of one's acts. By doing so, one can act inconsistently with one's foundational attitude but reduce the risk of losing the benefits it provides. Since there will be situations in which this is a profitable course of action and since people are capable of rationalizing for their own benefit, we will observe instances in which people rationalize reflexively.

The third prediction is that there will be a correlation between being a rationalizing moral agent and having the normal human capacity to carry out projects that are in the agent's long-term interest. As we have seen, foundational attitudes originated because they improved an agent's ability to carry out projects that were in his long-term interest. Morality is a by-product of this adaptation. Because the two are inextricably linked, morality is maintained despite the fact that it is disadvantageous. It is maintained because it is linked to an advantageous adaptation. So if the theory is right, then anyone who is amoral will be bad at carrying out long-term projects and anyone who is bad at carrying out long-term projects will be amoral. Finding significant numbers of non-rationalizing and competent amoralists would prove that the theory is false. There is no guarantee that we will find any incompetent amoralists, however. If evolutionary intuitionism is true and if foundational attitudes have reached fixation, which is the situation in which every member of a species has a characteristic, every human being will be a competent moral agent. We are in luck insofar as the availability of evidence goes, as the following sections will show.

UNIVERSALITY

Donald Brown notes that all societies "distinguish right from wrong, and at least implicitly ... recognize responsibility and intentionality."[7] The universality of morality is confirmed to the extent that there are no societies that are obviously amoral: there may be societies that have amoral members but there are no amoral societies. There may be societies that have implausible moral codes, or even repugnant ones, but there are no societies without a moral code.

There is the occasional claim to the contrary. The most famous example of a supposedly amoral society is the Ik of Uganda. Colin Turnbull contends that the Ik, who were enduring a famine when he observed them, lack anything that could be called "morality."[8] But Turnbull himself describes behaviour that indicates the possession of a moral code and the existence of a moral sensibility. To give one example, he notes that those Ik who had been helped by others felt obligated to the helpers. More generally, serious questions about Turnbull's scholarship were raised by the linguist, Berndt Heine, who visited the Ik in the early 1980s.[9] He discovered, among other things, that Turnbull could not speak the language and mistook an ethnically mixed settlement for a purely Ik one. Heine notes that the Ik were reluctant to talk to him because of their anger at Turnbull's earlier portrayal of them. When first told about what had been written about them, the Ik had wanted to know whether they could take legal action against Turnbull. Hence, the Ik are not a clear counter-example to the claim that morality is universal.

THE OCCURRENCE OF REFLEXIVE RATIONALIZATION

Reflexive rationalization is not just a theoretical phenomenon. In one case, an anthropologist observed that a "woman who was in fact copying the designs of other potters with only the smallest variation was unaware that she copied, condemned copying as wrong, and had a strong conviction that she was in fact inventive and creative."[10] The woman had little talent, but because she wanted to make pots with original designs, she unconsciously altered her beliefs about what she was doing. This enabled her to continue copying while maintaining her belief that copying was wrong. She believed falsely but maintained the consistency of her beliefs.

Although she did not fool others, her reflexive rationalization was successful because she fooled herself.

There is more than just anecdotal evidence that people rationalize when they have no prudential reason for doing so. Consider people who affirm the moral code of their society when apparently speaking sincerely but who do not act in accordance with it. They tend to rationalize their discordant actions even though they have nothing to gain from making excuses to others. The same is true of people who do not act in accordance with their conception of themselves as good people. Sykes and Matza found that delinquents do not adhere to a non-standard moral code but neutralize their infractions of the standard code by means of excuses.[11] While not achieving all that its early proponents claimed for it, while not demonstrating that we always strive for consistency, Festinger's theory of cognitive dissonance[12] can explain rationalizations intended to protect the rationalizer's concept of himself as a person worthy of the respect of others.[13] In addition, there is a positive correlation between *self-reported* delinquency and the acceptance of typical excuses for criminal acts.[14] A prudent delinquent would not admit to his criminal acts in the first place if he had not already been caught. And someone who has already been caught appears to have nothing to gain and frequently stands to lose a great deal by rationalizing and maintaining the rationalization. For instance, some convicts are not paroled because they do not show remorse. It is unlikely that all remorseless convicts have been wrongly convicted. Therefore, it seems likely that some persist in their rationalizations even though they have been caught, even though others reject their "excuses," "explanations," and "justifications," and even though there would be obvious benefits to their surrendering their rationalizations.

Another piece of evidence for reflexive rationalization is that people who harm others tend to lower their opinion of them after they have harmed them.[15] In other words, being a victim results in a lowering of one's status in the view of the victimizers. This is a surprising phenomenon. The victimizers may have been carried away by events. They may have suffered from weakness of the will. But the recognition that they have done wrong can be detrimental to their functioning. One way of reducing their cognitive dissonance is by disparaging their victims. If their victims "deserved" what happened to them, then the perpetrators cannot be such bad people after all. If foundational attitudes are important for people's functioning and if believing truly about one's actions would impair the functioning that depends on them, this is just the sort of thing that one would expect. Others may not believe the rationalizers, but there is still a reason for the rationalizers to delude themselves.

MORALITY AND THE ABILITY TO CARRY OUT LONG-TERM PROJECTS

If foundational attitudes are the basis of morality, people will normally develop into moral agents who tend to rationalize reflexively in order to maintain consistency and their good opinion of themselves when they do not act morally. That is, they will normally develop into *rationalizing moral agents*. They will also normally develop into agents who are capable of planning, carrying out, and preserving the fruits of projects that are in their long-term interests: they will develop into *planners*. If possessing a foundational attitude is what makes a rationalizing moral agent with a capacity for planning, then there will be a strong positive correlation between being a rationalizing moral agent and being a planner.

There are people who are neither rationalizing moral agents nor planners: psychopaths. They are the only identifiable group of deviants who are diagnosed as being both subjectively and objectively amoral. Psychotics, for instance, are not subjectively amoral and are no more inclined to objective amorality than normal human beings, to judge by their propensity to commit violent crimes involving victims who do not figure in their delusions.[16] But the psychopath is without a conscience. "Psychopaths show a stunning lack of concern for the devastating effects their actions have on others. Often they are completely forthright about the matter, calmly stating that they have no sense of guilt, are not sorry for the pain and destruction they have caused, and that there is no reason for them to be concerned."[17] Psychopaths may concoct excuses in order to avoid punishment, but they have no psychological commitment to them. They are adept at this sort of prudential rationalization. Their ability may be explained partly by the absence of internal constraints on the rationalizations they put forth. Since their rationalizations are devised only to enable them to escape sanctions of some sort, they will not persist in them if they see that there is no prudential advantage in doing so. When they rationalize, they are not their own audience. They do not rationalize reflexively.

Not only are psychopaths amoral, but they are also bad at planning, carrying out, and preserving the fruits of projects that are in their long-term interests. Hervey Cleckley, the pioneering researcher into psychopathy, makes this clear. The psychopath "does not maintain an effort to any far goal at all. This is entirely applicable to the full psychopath. On the contrary, he seems to go out of his way to make a failure of life. By some incomprehensible and untempting piece of folly or buffoonery, he eventually cuts short any activity in which he is succeeding, no matter whether it is crime or honest endeavor."[18] "He throws away excellent opportunities to make money, to achieve a rapprochement with his wife, to be dismissed from the hospital, or to gain other ends that he has sometimes spent considerable effort toward gaining."[19] Psychopaths throw away opportunities by indulging in debauches or by switching to some other goal. This behaviour is consistent with the development of other, stronger and incompatible desires such that attempts to satisfy them disrupt the efforts of psychopaths to secure their long-term interests. Psychopaths do sometimes try to achieve goals that are in their long-term interests, but they lack the ability to do so that ordinary people possess. They "feel that the easy scheme, the one-shot deal, or the clever ambush is much to be preferred over day-to-day commitment to a job, a long-term goal or a plan. Even when [psychopaths] are found in high-status jobs, these positions tend to be those in which the amount of actual hard work done (or not) can be easily obscured, or where others can be manipulated into being the real workers."[20] Cleckley listed a fairly large number of characteristics of psychopaths. Factor analysis has reduced this to two: a disregard for the future and a disregard for moral considerations.[21]

The characteristics are not independent of each other. Psychopaths are a subset of people with antisocial personality disorder. Swanson, Bland, and Newman found that 3 percent of the population of Edmonton had recently exhibited the symptoms of antisocial personality disorder and that 3.7 percent had exhibited them at some time in their lives.[22] Robins, Tipp, and Przybeck estimated the lifetime prevalence of antisocial personality disorder to be 4 percent.[23] According to Hart and Hare, "anywhere between 50% and 80% of offenders and forensic patients are diagnosed as [having antisocial personality disorder], whereas only about 15% to 30% of the same people [are psychopaths]."[24] Hare and others argue that the criteria used to define antisocial personality disorder leave out the freedom of the psychopath from shame, guilt, and remorse.

If we know how many people are psychopaths, we know how many people are neither rationalizing moral agents nor planners. Hence, we can estimate how many would be rationalizing moral agents but not planners and how many would be planners but not rationalizing moral agents if the characteristics were independent. If 80 percent of the criminally inclined have antisocial personality disorder but just 15 percent of them are psychopaths, then about 19 percent of the criminally inclined with antisocial personality disorder will be psychopathic. If the ratio can be extrapolated to the population as a whole and if 3 percent of the general population exhibit antisocial personality disorder, just over 0.5 percent of the general population will be psychopathic. If 0.5 percent of the population is psychopathic and if the traits are independent, there should be an average of about 7 percent of the population in each of the two categories – 7 percent of 7 percent is 0.49 percent. Obviously, even when we make very conservative assumptions, the numbers are not there. The existence of 7 percent of the population with one characteristic or the other could not go unnoticed. Isolated examples of good-hearted people who are disorganized or of wicked people who pursue long-term goals with determination do not justify denying that there is a positive correlation between being a rationalizing moral agent and being a planner because the argument is statistical. Chance alone will ensure that there are *some* successful psychopaths.

There is in fact no evidence of significant numbers of people who are rationalizing moral agents but who are not planners. They would lack the psychopath's proclivity for criminal or callous acts, but they would otherwise have the same lifestyle as the psychopath. "Psychopaths tend to live day-to-day and to change their plans frequently. They give little serious thought about the future and worry about it even less."[25] There do not appear to be many such people who are not psychopaths. Naturally, there are people whose objective situation is such that long-term projects are counterproductive or a waste of time, but they do not constitute counter-examples. There are also cases in which people's plans fail. However, there are few, if any, cases in which someone forfeits a great good that he has worked long and hard to achieve by performing a good but insignificant act. Nobody loses a job or misses a test because he is doing things such as running errands for a neighbour who is down with a minor but not incapacitating illness. Moreover, people do not rationalize going to work or writing exams instead of running trivial errands.

There also appear to be few if any people who are not psychopathic and who do not rationalize their pursuit of their self-interest at the expense of others. Whenever we examine the case of someone who appears to be amoral and capable of successful long-term planning, we find some sort of rationalization. Predatory "entrepreneurs" may admit that they are acting without much regard for the interests of others. They may also couple the admission with a crude variant of Adam Smith's notion of the "invisible hand" and its benefits and conclude that acting in a self-interested manner is positively virtuous. Some may see themselves as better than others because they are "realistic" and not hypocritical. Others may act immorally within a certain sphere of activity because they hold that morality does not extend into the sphere, which is a way of rationalizing kinds of acts rather than individual acts. Some may excuse themselves by saying that *everybody* does it. This would constitute what appears to be social proof that their actions are permissible. The straightforward occurrence of objective wrongdoing does not refute the claim that planners rationalize. Only sincerely admitted subjective wrongdoing without remorse on the part of people who are capable of successfully completing long-term projects would do so. Naturally, sincerely admitted subjective wrongdoing cannot involve merely an admission that one has done what is widely regarded by others as wrong, and it cannot be accompanied by a self-serving rationalization. The rational, calculating, and successful subjective amoralist is a creature of fiction.

The evidence is consistent with a strong positive correlation between someone's being a rationalizing moral agent and being capable of planning, carrying out, and preserving the fruits of projects that are in his long-term interest. But some objections are worth examining.

There may be apparent differences in the incidence of the behavioural symptoms of psychopathy from country to country, but they would not necessarily be good evidence that there is no connection between psychopathy and the possession of foundational attitudes. First, if some countries had a higher rate, the differences would be significant only if the populations were not self-selected to any great extent. If, for example, immigration or emigration had significantly altered the population profiles of some countries and if psychopaths were not averse to migrating, we should expect more psychopaths in countries with fewer social or political constraints on the lives of their citizens. Second, there may be differences in the behaviour of psychopaths in different societies even though roughly the same proportion of the population in every society is genetically psychopathic and has the potential to engage in such behaviour. Although there is some positive evidence that there is a genetic component to psychopathy[26] and a genetic component behind delinquency and criminality,[27] genetic explanations are compatible with social ones. "All that needs to be assumed in order to make these positions compatible is that people vary – largely for genetic reasons – in their abilities and inclinations to learn some behavior patterns more readily than others."[28] Needless to say, whatever an individual's predispositions to learn certain behaviour patterns, the number of opportunities to learn them may vary from society to society.

Psychopathy appears to admit of degrees whereas people either have or do not have foundational attitudes. But this also does not refute the hypothesis that most human beings have foundational attitudes. For one thing, the strength of foundational attitudes may vary, just as the strength of beliefs varies. Someone with a weak foundational attitude, one that did not provide him with much capacity to resist desires to perform content-inconsistent actions, would be more prone to suffer from weakness of the will. Furthermore, someone with a good ability to rationalize would find it easy enough to evade the obstacle provided by the moral code he espouses. Someone with a weak foundational attitude, strong desires, and a good ability to rationalize would act a lot like a psychopath. Since there are probably such near-psychopaths as well as true psychopaths, the best way to try to show that there is no correlation between planning and rationalization is to show that there are significant numbers of rationalizing moral agents who are not planners, that is, people whose lifestyle resembles that of psychopaths except for the criminality and callous use of others. As I have already indicated, there do not appear to be significant numbers of such people.

It does not follow that psychopathy is simply the absence of a foundational attitude. Perhaps psychopaths lack a precondition for the development of foundational attitudes. The correlation between being a rationalizing moral agent and being a planner would remain if psychopathy were explained in this way. It would be a better explanation than the alternative because the lack of a foundational attitude is not sufficient to explain all the characteristics of psychopaths. It does not, for instance, explain why they are not truly affectionate.

CONCLUSION

I have described a series of transitional forms that have culminated in organisms with foundational attitudes who are committed to regarding all other actual and potential possessors of the same type of attitude as valuable*. Each stage in the series is an improvement on what preceded it in terms of fitness. The final arrangement provides a basis for human morality. In no case, however, have I justified hypothesizing a feature just because it leads to a more plausible morality. On the contrary, each feature provides an evolutionary advantage that has nothing to do with morality. Hence, in the case of evolutionary intuitionism, the evolutionary story of the development of morality is an account of a by-product, not an adaptation. The story has three major empirical implications, which observation confirms. The confirmed predictions give us reason to believe that there really are foundational attitudes and that morality is a by-product of them, proving that evolutionary intuitionism is not just speculation. The next question is whether the existence of foundational attitudes could result in human morality. I shall start answering it by examining the normative ethics that we get when we base morality on foundational attitudes.

4

The Moral Facts According to Evolutionary Intuitionism

DISCOVERING MORAL FACTS

If evolutionary intuitionism is true, to act in a morally acceptable way is to act consistently with desire-dependent extended foundational attitudes. By determining what is consistent with them, we can determine what is morally permissible. Moreover, as I shall argue in chapter 6, our intuitions must correspond to the moral facts when we possess all relevant true beliefs and no relevant false beliefs because the moral facts are part of the causal explanation for our intuitions. If the facts and our intuitions were profoundly at variance, evolutionary intuitionism would be falsified. Hence, determining whether the theory gives us intuitively acceptable results is a way of testing the theory.

Although the theory is not falsified by the results, it does not follow that no one will take exception to them. The correspondence between the results of the theory and our actual intuitions has to be reasonably good. It does not have to be perfect because imperfection could be the result of ignorance, error, or reflexive rationalization. It is difficult for people to eliminate the influence of these factors on their intuitions. Hence, the results can go against our intuitions to some extent without putting the theory in serious doubt. Moreover, a modicum of counter-intuitiveness is tolerable, because the empirical evidence for the theory, as set out in chapter 3, offsets and outweighs it.

I am not advancing a moral principle or set of principles from which, in conjunction with factual premises, we can derive specific moral judgments. Rather, I am describing what would be the case if moral facts were constituted by the relations between acts and foundational attitudes. Nonetheless, it is possible to describe the moral facts in general terms using terminology that is appropriate to moral theories that posit principles. This, however, is just a *façon de parler.*

Speaking in that manner, I would describe what evolutionary intuitionism gives us as a consequentialism with deontological side-constraints. In other words, if it were possible to devise a moral theory consisting of moral principles, then that theory would be a deontologically limited consequentialism. It would be a consequentialism that would have us minimize premature death and significant injury but not by whatever means that would produce that end. The desire-dependence of a person's foundational attitude limits the ways in which he can be committed to act. The limitations are absolute and cannot be outweighed by the fact that some larger number of other persons could be preserved from significant injury if someone sacrificed himself, say. One cannot have an obligation when the grounds for it have vanished. However, the fact that some ways of minimizing injury are not obligatory does not eliminate the requirement on us to minimize. Only occasionally does the prohibition of some means of minimizing significant injury prevent us from minimizing as much as we could if no way of achieving the end were prohibited.

I am not going to tease out every implication of the theory. I will merely explore its implications sufficiently to illuminate the full range of factors relevant to the moral facts and to demonstrate that certain indubitably counter-intuitive consequences do not follow. I will use the terminology introduced in chapter 2 in connection with moral facts. An act is content-consistent if and only if it is consistent with the content of an agent's foundational attitude. It is desire-compatible if and only if the agent can perform it while, in order of importance, desiring to avoid significant injury to himself, desiring to preserve his kin, etc., and desiring to preserve his friends.

MINIMIZATION

The consequentialism of evolutionary intuitionism is not constrained deontologically in every set of circumstances. Here I will consider when it is not so constrained, when people can act both content-consistently and desire-compatibly. Obviously, possessors of foundational attitudes have a prima facie obligation to minimize the loss of what they are committed to take to be of value*,[1] because the mere fact that something is of value* provides a reason not to destroy it and a reason to preserve it from destruction. If there is a single other possessor of a foundational attitude to be preserved, a moral agent has a reason to preserve him. If there are two, he has a reason to preserve them both. If there are three, he must preserve three. If there are more than he has the ability and resources to save, it follows nonetheless that he has a reason to preserve as many as he has the ability and the resources to save and is in a position to save. If he fails to preserve one whom he had the ability and resources to save and whom he was in a position to save, then it is as though only one were in danger and he had failed to save him. Similarly, he is prima facie committed to minimize any damage that makes it more probable that someone else with a foundational attitude will die. If a possessor were not committed to minimize such damage to others with foundational attitudes, he would not be committed to minimize their destruction either.

The principle of minimization cannot be translated into a principle of maximization, because it is a function of a person's relationships to actually existing others, not of their possessing quanta of value*. Once someone has acknowledged at least one other possessor as being of value*, he has the same relevant relationship to a multiplicity of others: he must attribute value* to each of them; each of them has a claim to be a moral beneficiary of his in virtue of the relationship. No one has a commitment to increase the number of his potential moral beneficiaries, however. Possibly existing others simply do not come into the question.[2] When we talk about possibly existing others, there is in fact no one with whom a possessor has the relevant relationship.

We are not committed to "satisfice" rather than minimize either: saving a large enough number of other people does not relieve us of the obligation to save even more if more are in danger. This is also a consequence of the relations between actual and potential possessors of foundational attitudes. If someone were committed to save just enough possessors or potential possessors and free not to save the rest, then his relation to the latter would be different from his relation to the former. But he has the same relevant relation to them all and is committed to regard them all as valuable* and to act accordingly. Acting accordingly in some cases does nothing to alter the agent's commitments in other cases.[3]

Because of our limited abilities when acting as individuals, we may be committed to co-operating with others. For instance, if a shipload of orphaned and deserted children was discovered off the coast, a person would have an obligation to feed, clothe, and house them, everything else being equal. Other people would have the same obligation. If two people could do more by co-operating than they could accomplish by acting independently, each would be committed to co-operate with the other in caring for the orphans. Although someone who was not capable of caring for all the needs of one of the orphans would have an excuse for not taking complete responsibility, it does not follow that he would have no responsibility at all. Moreover, even if just one person with a foundational attitude were capable of caring for one of the orphans, others would not cease to be committed to preserve him. They would still have some responsibility.

It follows that we have obligations to establish institutions that minimize the loss of what we are committed to take to be of value*. Commitments to act co-operatively with others exist because of our commitment to preserve others, the needs of those others, and our limitations as individuals. Success is often more probable if we institutionalize our efforts and if some of us specialize in performing specific kinds of work within the institutions we create. The required institutions can be local ones such as hospitals, regional ones such as medical schools, national ones such as medicare systems, or international ones such as aid programs.

In one sort of case, the need to minimize loss of what we are committed to take to be of value* would require us to bring about the deaths of other possessors. This is the case in which the ones who die are a proper subset of the set of those who would otherwise die and in which there are no less drastic measures that could be taken to achieve the same end. For instance, if ten temporarily unconscious non-swimmers were in a sinking boat and if the boat would remain above the water if there were only nine in it, it would be absurd to let them all drown instead of removing one and letting him drown.

DEONTOLOGICAL CONSTRAINTS ON MINIMIZATION

The primary deontological constraints on minimization are imposed by the desire-dependence of foundational attitudes. No one is ever committed to perform a desire-incompatible act, not even if only such an act would minimize loss of value*. It is impossible for such a commitment to arise. We must minimize, but some ways of achieving that end are not required, and others are forbidden.

Obviously, there are causal processes that endanger possessors and potential possessors but in which no possessors are caught up. In these cases, everyone is free to prefer himself to his family, his family to his friends, and his friends to strangers when it is not possible to preserve all. In some situations, since everyone has a prima facie obligation to minimize loss of what he is committed to take to be of value*, everyone has some duties first to his kin, second to his friends, and third to strangers. No one is required to treat strangers as though they were family or friends in such situations. Consequently, if one must choose between saving a friend from drowning and saving a stranger, one must save one's friend. Or, if one can grow food and either give it to one's family to preserve them or give it to strangers, one must feed one's family first. But the freedom to put family and friends first when there is a conflict between their needs and the needs of strangers does not eliminate the requirement to help strangers when there is no conflict. Once we have taken care of our families and our friends, we must look to the well-being of others. The fact that we may *sometimes* put some before others does not alter the thrust of the requirement to minimize loss of value*.

The deontological constraints on minimization have another, more interesting and potentially controversial consequence. It is always permissible to intervene in causal processes that would otherwise result in significant injury to oneself or in one's death. Intervention to secure self-preservation is permissible no matter whether it causes the deaths of villainous aggressors, innocent aggressors, innocent threats, or those simply caught up in the causal processes. An example of people caught up in causal processes that would harm an agent would be provided by people caught up in an avalanche that threatens the agent. They are not the threat; the avalanche is. The agent could save himself by diverting the avalanche even if his action resulted in the deaths of the people caught up in it. The only proviso would be that the death-causing intervention would indeed be necessary for self-preservation. Someone who refrained from attempting to preserve himself in this kind of situation would have to desire something more than he desired to avoid significant injury to himself.

These constraints do not provide a license to kill in order to preserve oneself. It is not morally permissible for someone to kill others in order to save his own life unless they are aggressors, threats, or those caught up in causal processes that pose a threat to him. For instance, cannibalism is not permitted during a famine even if someone could survive only by becoming a cannibal, because a person can both refrain from killing the innocent and *desire* to avoid significant injury at least as much as anything else. A person's foundational attitude depends on his being able to *desire* to avoid significant injury, *not* on his being able to *satisfy* the desire. His desire to avoid injury could be his strongest desire, his foundational attitude could be intact, and he could nevertheless be committed not to act in the only way in which he could satisfy his desire to avoid injury. He would not have to have a desire stronger than his desire to avoid significant injury in order to refrain from killing in these cases. What would prevent him, if it did prevent him, would be his foundational attitude, not a desire.

The point of view of a participant is not interchangeable with the point of view of an observer. No one is committed to suffer significant injury at the hands of villainous aggressors or to suffer it in order to preserve innocent aggressors or innocent threats or those caught up in causal processes that endanger him. If need be, *he* is free to preserve himself. Others acting on his behalf do not have the same liberty. Although they are free to kill villainous aggressors if need be and circumstances warrant, as I shall argue later, they are almost never free to bring about the deaths of the innocent or to cause significant harm to them. (I will discuss a couple of exceptions later.) A person is free to preserve *himself* in all four cases because it would be desire-incompatible for *him* to act otherwise, but it would not be desire-incompatible for others to refrain from saving him in any of the cases. Their foundational attitudes are not dependent on *his* being able to desire to avoid significant injury more than anything else.

Similar conclusions can be reached with respect to the other forms of desire-dependence. A person may interfere in causal processes that would harm his family or friends, but he may not kill people who do not threaten them or who are not caught up in causal processes that threaten them even though doing so would benefit them. Killing others for food during a famine so that one's family or friends will survive is no more permissible than killing others to feed oneself in the same circumstances. The point of view of a participant is still not interchangeable with the point of view of an observer.

The idea that a person is free to kill innocents caught up in processes that endanger him may appear counter-intuitive, especially when someone kills many others in order to save himself. It is true that the greater the disparity between potential losses, the more it seems that we should choose the smaller loss: it is always better to lose less. Someone who actively or passively sacrificed himself in the sorts of situations described would be admirable. However, in these cases, our intuitions are over-generalizations.

A number of things can be said to soften the blow. First, the same sorts of problems occur in connection with other deontological theories. In addition, this theory is less extreme than some others. It forbids us to trade lives for lives. Kant forbids us to trade lies for lives. Second, we would find ourselves on a slippery slope, where we would be forced to accept smaller and smaller disparities until we reached the conclusion that it was obligatory to sacrifice a whole person to prevent one death and one cut finger, say. We would end up concluding that we could never intervene in causal processes to save ourselves, our families, or our friends if our intervention harmed others. These conclusions are not only themselves counter-intuitive but are also inconsistent with our nature as biological creatures. Third, if we were committed to sacrifice ourselves, it seems probable that we would be permitted to sacrifice a small number of others in order to save a large numbers of others and that they would be committed to submit to being sacrificed. But that conclusion is counter-intuitive as well. If there is one thing that many people are intuitively certain of, for instance, it is that people should not be used as sources of spare parts in surgical procedures, even if using them that way would save a larger number of lives. I will argue shortly that we are committed to avoid that sort of thing.

Finally, if morality is evolutionary in origin, then conceivably there will be unusual or extreme circumstances in which it will fail to provide an answer about the right course of action. Evolutionary adaptations are frequently inferior to what an engineer would design, and morality is not even an adaptation. It would hardly be surprising if a morality produced by evolution turned out to be more limited than a moral philosopher with a bent for the fantastic would like it to be. Outside philosophical fiction, however, it is rare to find either cases in which sacrificing one person will save many other people or cases in which self-preservation requires intervening in causal processes in such a way that the deaths of innocents occur. Such cases would have been exceedingly rare in the environment of evolutionary adaptation, in the small-scale societies in which human beings lived throughout most of their evolutionary history. Of course, if morality is limited in this way, people could create situations in which morality fails to provide answers: sophisticated sadists could confront people with insoluble dilemmas as a way of tormenting them. But it does not follow that evolutionary intuitionism is false or that it can be replaced by a better theory.

WHY INVOLUNTARY SACRIFICES ARE WRONG

Desire-dependence means that no one is obligated to suffer significant injury. It is also the case that everyone is obligated to avoid sacrificing another against the other's will if the sacrifice would involve significant injury. Suppose that some people sacrificed another person without his consent. There are four relevant points of view: those of the victim, the beneficiaries, the bystanders, and the perpetrator(s). "Beneficiaries" is in the plural because if the victims outnumbered the beneficiaries, the sacrifice would be wrong on consequentialist grounds alone. The crux of the problem is the question of what it is permissible for the perpetrators to do. I will examine the case from the perspectives of the other participants first, however.

First, the victim would have to regard the sacrifice of himself as wrong. If we assume that someone with a foundational attitude is obligated to sacrifice himself, we get a *reductio ad absurdum*. The victim is also free to preserve himself, even at significant cost to others, as I argued above. Therefore, he is free to refuse to be sacrificed no matter how much might be gained through his sacrifice. Indeed, in order to preserve his own life, he is free to kill those who would sacrifice him.[4] Regarding himself as being of value*, desiring to avoid significant injury, and rightfully believing that he could take drastic measures to defend himself, he would inevitably regard his victimization as wrong.

Second, the beneficiaries are committed not to countenance the sacrifice of another for their sake. If they consented to someone's being sacrificed for their sake, their desires to avoid significant injury would not be outweighed, and their foundational attitudes would be intact. Just as they themselves are committed not to kill those who are not involved in causal processes that endanger them in order to preserve themselves, they are committed not to countenance the deaths of those whom others would kill on their behalf. They would have to regard the sacrifice as wrong.

Third, bystanders would see this as a case of sacrificing someone not involved in the causal processes that endanger the beneficiary. Their foundational attitudes would be intact, and they too would be committed not to countenance the sacrifice.

As for the perpetrators, there are two possibilities: one in which their foundational attitude is "on" and one in which it is "out." In the first case, they would be committed not to sacrifice the victim. If they were not, they would be committed to countenance others sacrificing them (because they sacrificed someone) and not to countenance others sacrificing them (because they retained their foundational attitudes), which is absurd. In the second case, the perpetrator would have to have a desire that is stronger than his desires to preserve himself, his family, or his friends. He would desire to perform the sacrifice, and he might actually perform it, but he would no longer be subject to the influence of his foundational attitude, because it is desire-dependent. Naturally, he would be committed not to sacrifice the victim both before and after he was motivated by the desire that was stronger than his desires to preserve himself, his family, or his friends. If he made a moral judgment when in the grip of an over-powering desire to sacrifice one person for the sake of others, it would have to be by imagining what someone with a functioning foundational attitude would say. He would have to judge that it would be wrong to sacrifice the victim for the sake of the beneficiaries. Therefore, anyone who is capable of making a moral judgment would judge that sacrificing some for others was wrong. Everyone who was not in the grip of what would appear to be a fit of moral madness would be committed not to countenance such a sacrifice. All possessors of foundational attitudes that are "on" are committed not to sacrifice involuntary victims or to consent to their sacrifice. One cannot rationally and dispassionately decide to sacrifice an involuntary victim after a sober consideration of the morally relevant factors.

From every morally relevant point of view, it is impermissible for some to sacrifice another for yet others. It follows that everyone is free to disrupt an involuntary sacrificial arrangement even if the death of the prospective beneficiary results.[5] Going even further, since knowingly failing to disrupt an involuntary sacrificial arrangement when one could disrupt it constitutes consent, everyone is obligated to disrupt involuntary sacrificial arrangements.

Sacrificial arrangements sometimes occur naturally. These are cases in which continued pregnancy would kill or significantly injure a woman. The woman has the right to preserve herself even if the only means of doing so is killing the fetus. She has the right to refuse to die or be injured for its sake even if she became pregnant voluntarily. Women who become pregnant voluntarily do not expect that they will be injured. If it turns out that continued pregnancy would injure a woman significantly, she is free to terminate it.

Since it is permissible for a woman not to sacrifice herself, we are permitted to disrupt the involuntary sacrificial arrangement if the woman wants to escape it. It is permissible, indeed obligatory, for a knowledgeable and capable third party to perform an abortion when a woman in danger from continued pregnancy requests one. This is not a case in which the fetus is merely an innocent threat and in which we have not only an obligation to save the threatened but also an obligation not to do so by harming the threat. The dependence of the fetus on its mother makes the difference. If the threat posed by the fetus could be removed by removing it from its mother's body and if both the mother and the fetus would survive in a healthy state, then there would be no moral problem. When that option is not available even in principle because of the dependence of the fetus, we are dealing with a sacrificial arrangement.

Of course, our freedom to disrupt involuntary sacrificial arrangements justifies abortion only when the mother is in danger of suffering at least significant injury from continued pregnancy. Abortion because the fetus was not of the desired sex, say, or because continued pregnancy had become inconvenient, cannot be justified by this theory. It will be remembered that we have to attribute value* to others throughout their existence, including during those periods before they acquire foundational attitudes, and that individuals seem to come into existence once the process of conception is complete.

Sometimes, we happen to have desires that are both stronger than our desire to avoid injury and incompatible with it. Someone may want to save another more than he wants to preserve himself in a situation in which saving the other requires his own death. A pregnant woman may want her child to live more than she herself wants to live. Like suicide, acting toward this end is permissible. Although the woman eliminates her foundational attitude by pursuing this goal, someone who killed her would still be a wrongdoer, because he would put her child at risk.[6]

Of course, a person who intends to sacrifice himself is free to withdraw his consent at any time up to the point of no return. If he could not withdraw his consent, he would be committed to act in a way that is desire-incompatible and no one can be required to do so. No promise or agreement to sacrifice oneself can be sufficiently binding to offset this freedom. No matter what institutions we create, we could not create the possibility of a commitment to honour an agreement that required a person to perform a desire-incompatible act. People always have the right to change their minds about sacrificing themselves. Since self-sacrifice is not obligatory, neither is helping another to sacrifice himself.

As for helping a person to sacrifice himself, the standpoint of the helpers is not the same as the standpoint of the volunteer. All have an obligation to prevent situations in which people sacrifice themselves from arising and to discourage self-sacrifice, because all are obligated to minimize damage to and destruction of other possessors. Indeed, assistance would be permissible only when the sacrificial volunteer was actually in the process of sacrificing himself. Only then would it be clear that his foundational attitude was "out" and that it was a permissible case of voluntary sacrifice. This consequence obviously precludes the development of a system that would allow people to offer themselves up as a source of spare parts for medical procedures when death or significant injury would result. It does not preclude doing things like donating a kidney, however. Organ donation involves risking one's life, not sacrificing it, and taking risks does not necessarily indicate that one's foundational attitude is extinguished. Since risks are sometimes unavoidable, we are not obligated to try to avoid them all. We will see next that we can also have obligations to take risks for the sake of others.

SIGNIFICANT INJURY AND RISK

A person's foundational attitude depends on its being possible for him to desire to avoid significant injury at least as much as anything else when he acts. This fact played a significant role in the arguments in the two previous sections. If it is to be fully understood, we need a criterion of significant injury. It is as unreasonable to believe that someone does not have to save another because he would suffer an insignificant injury as it is to believe that he must sacrifice his life for others. The question is where to draw the line on the continuum between the two extremes. We can define a significant injury as one that would appreciably impair normal functioning or that would appreciably increase the probability of death. (On this definition psychological, as well as physical, injuries are significant injuries if they result in a shorter life or in suicide.) But the definition does not help us much.

The best way to decide the question is in relation to people's ordinary risk-taking behaviour. It is impossible to avoid risk completely, and no one eschews all risk, although some are more risk-averse than others. Suppose that in pursuit of non-moral objectives in ordinary circumstances someone is willing to do things that have one chance in ten thousand of causing his death. He would be inconsistent if he was unwilling to do things just as risky to save the life of another, say. Thus, it would be inconsistent for someone to risk death on the road by speeding for the enjoyment of it but to refuse to risk death on the road by taking another to hospital at the same speed. It would also be inconsistent for someone to risk his life when hang-gliding but to be unwilling to take a quantitatively similar risk to save another's life. Now, if it is required that a person perform an act that has one chance in ten thousand of causing his death, it can also be required that he suffer an actual injury with the same probability of causing his death. The seriousness of the risk is the same in both cases. Of course, if someone is willing to take greater risks than other people for non-moral reasons, he will be committed to take greater risks than others for moral reasons as well. The standards of morally acceptable risk are not absolute but relative to individual risk-takers. Naturally, no one is committed to suffer an injury more serious than the one he prevents. Unless the injury prevented was more serious, it would be a case of redistributing, not reducing, loss of value*, and there is no merit in mere redistribution.

Someone's taking risks for pleasure or sport does not thereby indicate that he does not hold that he is of value*. For one thing, people who reflexively rationalize risky activities can maintain their foundational attitudes as well. For another, although this case is rarer, those who indulge in risky activities may desire to get a thrill more than they desire to avoid significant injury. In some cases, they may even have a specific desire to risk death, and that desire may be stronger than their desire to avoid significant injury. The foundational attitudes of such people would be "out" during their performance of the risky act. To show that an example of risk-taking for pleasure or sport was incompatible with the risk-taker's holding that he was of value*, we would have to describe a person who had a realistic appreciation of the dangers, who did not rationalize his risk-taking activity, who did not desire to do something more than to avoid significant injury, and who nonetheless took risks. Naturally, taking reasonable risks to secure the well-being of oneself or other possessors of foundational attitudes is consistent with holding that one is of value*.

Our attitude to risk does not indicate that we do not hold that we are of value*. We often act as though the unnecessarily risky activities of others are inconsistent with their being of value*. We try to provide accurate information about the risks, which is a way of countering reflexive rationalization; we advise risk-takers to take precautions; we regulate some sports. And we forbid some particularly dangerous activities, ones that no one would engage in without reflexive rationalization or a death wish. This is all that is appropriate if the foundational attitudes of some risk-takers are "out" when they seek their thrill or intentionally risk their lives. There are no moral grounds for our forbidding them to perform all risky acts any more than there are moral grounds for our forbidding them to commit suicide.

THE CONSEQUENCES OF EGALITARIANISM

Not all deontological constraints result from the desire-dependence of extended foundational attitudes. Some result from the fact we must regard all possessors of foundational attitudes as being of value* and as being of equal value* to ouselves. It is always wrong to intentionally inflict even insignificant mental or physical injury on another unless doing so is necessary to prevent a loss of value*. If anyone were permitted to deliberately inflict insignificant injury on another for his own reasons – in order to get a frisson of sadistic delight, say – the behaviour would entail that the victim was merely of instrumental value relative to him, which, in turn, would imply that the victim was not intrinsically valuable and, hence, not of value*. Therefore, intentionally causing insignificant injury for morally insufficient reasons is always wrong no matter how strongly the potential attacker desires to inflict it, because it violates out commitment to treat others as being of value*.

In addition, when there is a choice between acting in a way that involves treating some people as worth less than others and acting in a way that does not do so, we are committed to act in the latter way, even if no particular injury results. For instance, racially segregated washrooms with inferior fixtures in the facilities for the disfavoured would be intrinsically wrong even if the disfavoured were not psychologically damaged by the inferior status imposed on them. All are worthy of equal respect.

In fact, the only adequate moral justification for a privilege would be one that showed that the privilege is necessary to minimize the loss of what we are committed to take to be of value*. In other words, the only moral reason for privileging an individual would be that what he does is of instrumental value to yet other possessors of foundational attitudes and that his being privileged reduces loss of value*. For example, a case can be made that physicians should have the right to double park in emergencies.

Everything else being equal, it is no more important to satisfy the desires of one person than it is to satisfy the desires of another. In this case, the *ceteris paribus* clause indicates that the desires are content-consistent and of equal weight or significance. There may be particular cases in which satisfying one person's desire is more important than satisfying another's. However, there can be no general rule that the desires of some should outweigh the desires of others. If we are committed to attribute to other possessors of foundational attitudes the same amount of value* as we attribute to ourselves, always treating one person's desires as more important than another's is wrong, because doing so presupposes that the former is more valuable* than the latter.

Thus, we have a prima facie obligation to reform or abolish customs or institutions that promote unequal status, unequal treatment, or exploitation. For instance, the subjugation of women is wrong even if it is in the biological interest of males to subjugate them.

Despite this fundamental equality, however, even a hierarchy could be justified if it were necessary for the successful completion of a long-term project that was in the interests of those who contributed to it. For instance, a management hierarchy in a firm could be justified if the firm were a kind of long-term project. But a hierarchy must have strictly limited powers. In the case of the firm, it may have the powers it needs to operate the firm successfully, but it must not have the power to determine working conditions unilaterally or to control the private lives of workers. Because of the disparity in power, workers must have at the very least the right to organize into trade unions so that working conditions can be determined in negotiations between the workers and management on a basis of equality.

More egalitarian arrangements might be desirable, however. The details of arrangements often have to be worked out by the parties to them, whether the parties are workers and management or citizens and government, because the complexity of human societies, human relationships, and human interactions often make it difficult to determine the effects on equality of a custom or an institution. Outsiders are often unable to do more than to point out that institutions ought to be organized in the light of the need for moral equality, as well as productivity or efficiency.

Equality trumps economics. The economic costs of achieving equality are morally bearable unless they increase the probability of the deaths of some possessors of foundational attitudes. The currency of morality is human lives, human well-being,and human dignity. Other currencies are subordinate to it.

REACTING TO WRONGDOERS

Everyone has an obligation to prevent Cain from killing Abel when Cain has no good reason to kill him. If Cain's killing Abel is content-inconsistent, then our consenting to Cain's killing him is also content-inconsistent. If consenting to it is content-inconsistent, everyone is obligated to prevent it, provided that there is a way of doing so that is both content-consistent and desire-compatible. There is no neutrality in this kind of case: inaction is consent. Someone is free not to defend himself; he might desire something more than to avoid injury. But no one is free to ignore an attack on another. If anyone did, he would be committed to the inconsistent view that the victim was both valueless* and valuable*.

Some ways of preventing Cain's killing Abel are content-consistent. In fact, if the only way to do so is by killing Cain, then killing Cain is content-consistent. The content-consistency of killing him is a function of the fact that otherwise he would proceed in a content-inconsistent manner and consenting to that would be content-inconsistent as well.

However, we also have an obligation to use minimal force. If there are content-consistent ways of preventing Cain from killing Abel that do not involve killing Cain, then we must prevent the killing in one of those ways. Overpowering and disarming him is better than shooting him, because we are committed to minimize loss of value*, Cain's acting in a content-inconsistent way does not eliminate his foundational attitude, and we are committed to attribute value* to him.

Of course, not all possible ways of saving Abel are content-consistent. Even if we could save Abel by killing an innocent bystander, that action would be content-inconsistent. It is wrong to sacrifice some in order to prevent greater wrongdoing by others, for the same reasons that it is wrong to sacrifice them in other circumstances. It is also wrong to cause significant injury to them for that purpose. This is another respect in which the deontological nature of evolutionary intuitionism reveals itself.

Punishment after the fact is permissible. It might be possible to prevent Cain from killing Abel, not by intervening when the attack is in progress, but by threatening him with death in retaliation. If Cain kills Abel nonetheless, we are free to carry out the threat. If we were not, there would be some circumstances in which we would be committed to consent to a content-inconsistent act. Hence, we are free to kill Cain after he commits murder if it was reasonable to kill him in order to prevent him from committing murder in the first place. It does not matter that Cain has already succeeded in killing Abel, provided that we ensure that Cain's killing Abel really was a culpable homicide.

The seriousness of a content-inconsistent act places an absolute limit on how drastic the ways of preventing it may be. Killing another who is acting content-consistently is only one way of acting in a content-inconsistent manner. Another way is to treat people with foundational attitudes as though they were merely of instrumental value, rather than of value*. Degrading someone in this way is content-inconsistent, but it is not as serious as killing him, because the situation can be remedied and the degraded person can be compensated. Therefore, killing someone in order to prevent him from degrading someone else is itself content-inconsistent.

It follows that when justifying punishment, we must take into account not just whether the punishment is an adequate deterrent but also whether it is in proportion to the crime. There is a deontological limit to justifiable punishment, and exceeding it transforms a way of deterring one wrong into a second wrong. Not only are we faced with an absolute constraint on the permissible severity of punishment, a limit that depends on the seriousness of the content-inconsistent act, but we must also remain as far below the limit as possible while still preventing it. We must impose a lesser sanction if we have reason to think the threat of a less drastic response will be sufficient. We are committed to use "minimal force" in this kind of case also. Capital punishment is not forbidden in all circumstances but any lesser sanction that would deter to the same extent would be preferable. There are, of course, good reasons for developing institutions to deal with such cases, because institutionalized responses are more likely to deal with cases objectively and with proportionate punishment.

Threatening punishment is not the only way to respond to potential content-inconsistent acts. Whether a criminal is deterred appears to depend more on the probability of detection and arrest than on the severity of the punishment typically meted out.[7] Consequently, doing things to increase the probability that crimes will be detected and the culprits caught is preferable to increasing the severity of the threatened punishments, and not only preferable but also obligatory. Hence, if decentralized policing of the sort that exists in Japan makes crime less probable than does the centralized policing (combined with mobile patrols) that is the norm in many other countries, then the former should be introduced. Preventing crime is better than reacting to it.

Killing human shields is sometimes permissible. Because we are committed not to damage or destroy people who act in content-consistent ways, we are committed not to use an innocent bystander to shield ourselves from an attack. But if Cain used a bystander as a shield to carry out his attack on others and if Cain's tactic committed us to refrain from preventing his attack on the others, then we would be committed to consent to Cain's attack when carried out under those conditions. But consenting to Cain's attack would be content-inconsistent. Therefore, we are free to prevent Cain from attacking others even if we kill the human shield in the process, provided that the only way of preventing the attack involves destroying the human shield. We must not reach the conclusion that there is no alternative too quickly, and we must try every other way we reasonably can before acting in a way that results in the shield's death. A measure of desperation in our search for a way to prevent Cain from killing the others while saving the human shield is proper here.

So far, the wrongdoers under discussion have been people to whom we have no special relationship. But things do not change if the wrongdoer is a friend or a relative. Desire-dependence gives us the freedom to prefer friends or relatives to strangers when we cannot meet our obligations to all. Ordinary obligations, obligations to strangers, are lifted under those conditions, but obligations to friends and relatives are not. But the freedom to feed one's family rather than strangers does not entail that one has a special obligation to countenance wrongdoing on the part of friends or relatives. On the contrary, our obligations with respect to wrongdoing friends or relatives are the same as our obligations with respect to strangers. If we make allowances for their crimes, we become complicit in them. If we enable them to commit crimes, we share their guilt.[8] People may be disposed to favour their friends or relatives in circumstances other than those in which evolutionary intuitionism allows them to favour them: for example, parents may be inclined to conceal the crimes of their offspring. But they do not have a right to do so. Our natural inclinations, inclinations produced by variation and natural selection, are not always morally acceptable. Those that dispose us to act content-inconsistently are not virtues.

CONCLUSION

Evolutionary intuitionism makes some moral judgments true. The results to be obtained through discovering the moral facts are recognizably the same sort of results that normative moral theories give us. None is utterly implausible. All do well enough to pass the test of intuitiveness. But we do not always agree on moral matters or always act in morally acceptable ways. If foundational attitudes exist and if they influence our beliefs and behaviour, we must explain why we are not biologically predestined always to believe truly about moral issues or always to do the right thing. Evolutionary intuitionism faces obstacles in the motivational sphere, but in the next chapter I will argue that the obstacles can be surmounted.

5

Motivation, Evasion, and Variation

INTRODUCTION

The moral facts hypothesized by evolutionary intuitionism are obviously not the only factors influencing either our moral beliefs or our moral behaviour. Not all moral beliefs correspond to the hypothesized moral facts. People all too often do what is wrong if the facts are as evolutionary intuitionism describes them. On the other hand, the moral facts do have an influence. The problem is to distinguish the moral signals from the background noise. The aim of this chapter is to show that this can be done and that we can expect the background noise to be there.

EXISTENCE INTERNALISM, MORAL JUDGMENTS, AND MORAL MOTIVATION

Foundational attitudes are constituents of moral facts. What is important for the present discussion is that they are like beliefs when it comes to their relationship to action. We can predict actions if we know the agent's desires and beliefs. In order for us to predict actions, it must be the case that if someone believes a proposition and does not act in ways that are consistent with both it and its negation, then, *ceteris paribus*, he will act consistently with the proposition and inconsistently with its negation. It must be true that a believer is disposed not to act inconsistently with the propositions he believes. Foundational attitudes have the same sort of influence on our actions as beliefs do. Except in cases of weakness of the will, either we will act in ways that are consistent with them and believe truly about our actions, or we will act in ways that are inconsistent with them and maintain the consistency of our mental stocks of propositional attitudes by inaccurately describing our actions to ourselves.

This fact about foundational attitudes provides the basis for an account of moral motivation. I use the term "moral motivation" with misgivings because it may convey the impression that I am talking about an impulse to act morally. What I am actually describing is a sort of resistance to acting immorally if the agent acts. The resistance may be supplemented by an inculcated desire to act morally, but such a desire is not necessary on my account. Nevertheless, since it has become the standard expression, I shall persist in using "moral motivation."

Since internalism and externalism are mutually exclusive and jointly exhaustive of the possibilities, my account of moral motivation must be classified as internalist. Stephen Darwall distinguishes between "judgment internalism" and "existence internalism." The former posits a necessary connection between affirmations of moral judgments and motivation or between moral beliefs and motivation, at least under certain conditions, such as when the moral judge is fully rational. The latter claims that, necessarily, if it is the case that someone morally ought to do something, then he is motivated to do it. "According to *existence internalism*, someone morally (or ethically) ought to do something only if, necessarily, she (*the agent*) has (actually or dispositionally) motives to do so."[1]

The internalism of evolutionary intuitionism is a form of existence internalism. The agent's foundational attitude will prevent him from acting as he morally ought not to act in most situations. Consider someone with a foundational attitude who morally ought to do something, who possesses all relevant true beliefs and no relevant false ones, who has no inclination to rationalize reflexively, who does not suffer from weakness of the will, and who is motivated to act. He will be disposed to act as he morally ought to act because his foundational attitude will preclude any other course of action. Suppose that an act A is desire-compatible but content-inconsistent. Assume that other acts are available to the agent and that all of them are both content-consistent and desire-compatible. The act A is consistent with the negation of the proposition that the agent is of value*. If the agent has a foundational attitude, then it will incline him to perform acts that are consistent with his foundational attitude and inconsistent with its negation when he does not act in ways that are consistent with both. Hence, if he has a foundational attitude and if he acts for any reason at all, he will be disposed not to perform the act A, because it is consistent with the negation of his foundational attitude. If he acts, no matter the reason, he will perform one of the content-consistent and desire-compatible acts available to him. If there is only one content-consistent act available to him, he will perform that act, whatever he desires. Moral obligations are categorical imperatives, not hypothetical ones.

In this situation, the agent's true moral judgment that it is wrong for him to do A is also motivationally superfluous. If the agent makes the true moral judgment that it is wrong for him to perform A, his judgment will be true in virtue of the fact that doing A is content-inconsistent. His being disposed not to do A will be correlated with his moral judgment that it is wrong for him to do A. However, his moral judgment will not bring it about that he is disposed not to do A. The situation is analogous to one in which two events have a common cause. The events are correlated, but neither causes the other. The true moral judgment (analogous to one of the events) does not bring it about that the judge is motivated (analogous to the other event). Conversely, that the judge is motivated to act morally does not bring it about that he judges at all, let alone that he judges truly. True moral judgments and moral motivation are independent of one another.

To be completely accurate, it must be said that the true moral judgments of an agent with a foundational attitude will be correlated with moral motivation only when the moral agent is the subject of the judgment. He will be the subject of the judgment when it is one that *he*, the judge, makes concerning *his own* obligations. Moral judgments about another person in his situation will not be so correlated.[2] His foundational attitude will influence his behaviour in the appropriate way only when he is the subject of his own true moral judgments.

Moral judgments cannot replace foundational attitudes in the motivational scheme of things. People without foundational attitudes can make genuine moral judgments and remain unmoved by them. Someone without a foundational attitude could realize that doing A would be inconsistent with his having a foundational attitude, even though he lacked a foundational attitude. At the same time, he could realize that refraining from doing A would be compatible with his desiring to avoid significant injury at least as much as anything else, and so on. It is possible for him to express his apprehension of these facts by saying that doing A is wrong. In fact, someone who lacked a foundational attitude could use the same verbal formulas as someone with a foundational attitude in every case. Each could arrive at his conclusions by an independent consideration of the facts. Their respective conclusions would generally have the same truth-value.[3] Each could be as sincere as the other and equally firm in his conclusions. Each could believe his conclusions. However, someone who lacked a foundational attitude, unlike people with them, would have no natural resistance to acting in ways that were inconsistent with the proposition "I am of value*." If the reason for his performing an act were a moral reason, there would have to be an externalist explanation for his being morally motivated.

We may be tempted to think that people without foundational attitudes could not make genuine moral judgments, at least when an act would be desire-incompatible for them. It could be claimed that in order to make a genuine moral judgment in such cases, the judge would have to respond to the fact that performing the act would eliminate his foundational attitude. It could be claimed that it would not be enough for him to respond to the fact that performing it would be incompatible with his desiring to avoid significant injury at least as much as anything else, etc. But suppose a person with a foundational attitude responded to the fact that it was not possible for him to perform the act while desiring to avoid significant injury at least as much as anything else, and so on, and did not respond to the fact that his foundational attitude would be eliminated. The latter would surely be making a *moral* judgment. If not, it would follow that some people who possess foundational attitudes could not make genuine moral judgments either. Since there need be no difference between what a person with a foundational attitude and what someone without one would do, the latter could make a real moral judgment.

David Brink criticizes internalism on the ground that it makes the amoralist conceptually impossible. The amoralist is someone who can make a genuine moral judgment or have a genuine moral belief that an act is wrong but whose judgment or belief does not interfere with his performance of the act. Brink rejects the internalist counter that the amoralist is unmoved only by what is "*conventionally regarded* as moral."[4] I assume this means what others, but not the amoralist himself, believe to be moral. Brink characterizes the amoralist (as conceived by the internalist) as someone who can "recognize a moral consideration or assert a moral judgment and remain unmoved."[5] When Brink says that the amoralist remains unmoved, I take it that he means that the amoralist is not moved to act in what would be a morally acceptable way were his moral judgment correct. While it might affect judgment internalism, Brink's objection fails with respect to the existence internalism of evolutionary intuitionism. If my theory is true, there can be amoralists who make genuine, true moral judgments but who are not motivated to act in the way that people with foundational attitudes are.

ACTING MORALLY AND HOW WE AVOID IT

If acting morally is acting consistently with foundational attitudes and if we are so constructed that we tend not to act inconsistently with them, then acting morally is the default option. Therefore, the question that needs to be answered is how it is possible for people to act in morally unacceptable ways. There are several possible explanations.

People may simply possess relevant false beliefs or lack relevant true ones. They may act out of ignorance. For instance, people may harm others because they have false beliefs about the proper treatment for a condition from which the others suffer. Physicians who believed that bloodletting was beneficial did not intend to harm their patients.

Sometimes acts that would be objectively immoral if they were performed intentionally are performed unintentionally. People may act in ways that are inconsistent with their being of value* because they do not foresee, understand, or correctly estimate the probability of the consequences of their actions. In many cases, a later discovery of what they have done results in regret, remorse, and a desire to make amends. For example, someone who drives in a way that endangers others may discount the probability of his hurting someone else and may suffer tremendous remorse if he kills or injures someone.

In some rare instances, people do wrong by omission because they are so lacking in motivation that they have little inclination to do anything. Although people have a general disposition to have desires, that disposition can temporarily decline. Beliefs and foundational attitudes will not serve as a substitute source of motivation in the absence of desires, because they are motivationally inert in the absence of desires.

In other cases, people do wrong because they have a desire that is abnormally strong, stronger than the resistance of the foundational attitude opposing it. In these cases, people suffer from moral weakness of the will. For instance, sexual desire can overwhelm someone's conviction that it is wrong for him to impose himself sexually on others against their will, in which case he would be treating the other as being of instrumental value only. Alternatively and more rarely, weakness of the will may occur because people desire something more than they desire to avoid significant injury, as in the case of suicide bombers.

Finally, people do wrong objectively but maintain consistency by rationalizing reflexively. Reflexive rationalization is probably the most common enabling factor.

The various ways in which a person can end up acting other than content-consistently should make it clear that adopting evolutionary intuitionism does not presuppose biological determinism. Foundational attitudes may determine what we ought to do, but they are just one influence on what we actually do. While our capacity to acquire beliefs may be a biological adaptation, the particular beliefs we acquire are not. Since beliefs as well as foundational attitudes influence what we do and since beliefs are not products of evolution, our actions are not biologically determined.

THE USE OF REFLEXIVE RATIONALIZATION

People rationalize in order to maintain their good opinion of themselves. For example, someone who engages in petty sadism may describe his actions to himself as "teaching so and so a lesson" or, if he is in a position of authority, as "maintaining discipline." In these cases, at least part of the audience for the rationalization is obviously the rationalizer himself. This kind of rationalization is not intended to enable the rationalizer to avoid sanctions. If he is in a position of authority, he may not be subject to sanctions. But describing the violation of a moral rule inaccurately may enable a person to violate a rule that he accepts.

The truth is not an insurmountable obstacle to this kind of rationalization unless it is documented in some way and we are aware of the documentation. As is well known, our recollections naturally alter over time, often quite radically, as becomes obvious when more than one person recalls the same event and a dispute over the facts ensues. In the light of our fragmentary and ambiguous memories, we often unconsciously develop hypotheses to explain what "must" have happened. It is extremely easy to develop hypotheses that are as consistent as possible with one's image of oneself as a good person who is worthy of respect, or at least no worse than anyone else. It is also easy to develop hypotheses that are consistent with how one is now rather than how one was when one acted.[6]

A rationalization may take the form of a pseudo-description of the act, the form of a pseudo-justification or pseudo-excuse, including general grievances against others or attacks on one's victims, or the form of a list of spurious mitigating factors. When the sadist declares that he is just maintaining discipline, he fails to describe his actions accurately. When he declares that his victims deserve to be punished, but the punishment is disproportionate to the purported crime, he gives a pseudo-justification for his actions. When a shoplifter, in order to justify his thefts, claims that society is unjust and oppressive, he may be voicing nothing more than his resentment. When someone declares that he should not be blamed for something he did because he "was not himself," the mitigation is spurious.

Their reflexive rationalizations may not completely exonerate the wrongdoers. Sometimes, they will only reduce the seriousness of the acts somewhat or shift part of the blame to others. For instance, someone who assaults another may claim that he was deliberately provoked. In some cases, the rationalizer takes advantage of the fact that the same action can be explained by different sets of beliefs and desires. For instance, he may find it desirable to excuse his irrational anger with someone who fails at an assigned task by categorizing incompetence as sabotage.

Since people who do not have foundational attitudes will not have the same need to rationalize and since there are people who lack foundational attitudes, the occurrence of objective wrongdoing without rationalization does not show that human beings generally lack them any more than the occurrence of colour-blindness shows that people generally lack normal colour vision. Not every mature human being has a foundational attitude.

Reflexive rationalization can be retrospective or prospective. In cases of retrospective reflexive rationalization, people rationalize because the historical truth of what they have done is inconsistent with their foundational attitudes, they continue to hold that they are of value*, and they are inclined to maintain consistency. Retrospective reflexive rationalization is not inevitable when there are institutions that enable the wrongdoer to seek forgiveness or to make amends, with the ultimate aim of reintegrating him into the community. Without such a way out, however, the probability of retrospective reflexive rationalization is high. Prospective reflexive rationalization, which is a way of preparing to do wrong, is not as readily corrected. Institutional arrangements would not do as much to reintegrate the rationalizer, because institutions offer an alternative to reflexive rationalization and someone who rationalizes prospectively has already made his choice. Someone who kills another in a drunken brawl can have a choice between rationalizing the killing as a reasonable reaction to some sort of provocation and accepting responsibility for his act, showing contrition, making amends, and, consequently, being forgiven. Someone who plots to murder another for gain must rationalize his prospective crime beforehand and is unlikely to surrender the rationalization readily afterward.

There are two important corollaries. First, reflexive rationalization can motivate us to resist rational resolutions to moral disputes. Reflexive rationalizers will tend to resist any line of argument that is inconsistent with their rationalizations for the same reasons that they developed them in the first place. Second, some moral beliefs will be "fossils" whose existence is explained by the previous occurrence of reflexive rationalization. There will be moral opinions that persist despite the erosion of a necessary part of their original "justification" and that may therefore resemble raw intuitions. If people have acted in accordance with particular moral opinions, they will be motivated to maintain them because to do otherwise would be to admit that they had done wrong. Of course, they may invent new rationales for their beliefs. For example, people who no longer rely on scripture or outmoded biological theories to rationalize their antipathy towards homosexuals now claim that tolerance or acceptance of them somehow harms the family. The rationale has changed; the bigotry remains the same.

THE LIMITED USEFULNESS OF REFLEXIVE RATIONALIZATION

Some readers might worry that a person who was adept at rationalization would be more viable than one who was not and that, therefore, natural selection would eventually produce amoral people who were good at long-term projects. By rationalizing, the person would be able to escape the influence of his foundational attitude when acting content-inconsistently was to his advantage.

However, for several reasons reflexive rationalization has limited potential to enable immorality. First, the capacity to acquire true beliefs and to reject false ones previously acquired is itself generally adaptive. Reflexive rationalization impairs that ability. When they do not consist of beliefs that are accidentally true, rationalizations consist of false beliefs that bring other falsehoods in their wake. We are designed to respond to experience as "truth detectors," but developing a rationalization requires that we delude ourselves. There is liable to be tension. Second, it takes an effort to devise a rationalization. Indeed, it may be beyond a person's powers to devise a good one in some cases. There may not always be the leeway, or looseness of fit, necessary to ensure that our rationalizations are plausible. Third, when we rationalize reflexively, we are generally not conscious of doing so. Consequently, we have imperfect control over when we rationalize and the forms our rationalizations take. We risk rationalizing in ways incompatible with our securing our long-term interests.

Finally, if reflexive rationalizers who live in communities are detected, they may be liable to sanctions or risk being ostracized and losing the benefits that are accorded respectable members of communities of people with foundational attitudes. Ostracism would have been especially probable in the small-scale societies in which we lived throughout most of our evolutionary history, because everyone would have had an interest in others acting content-consistently when the actions of the others affected him or those whom he loved. Everyone has an interest in others being caught and penalized if they rationalize reflexively in order to escape their obligations. In short, people who rationalize reflexively risk losing the benefits of long-term co-operation with others. They are simultaneously trying to gain both the benefits that accrue to people who exhibit the symptoms of having a foundational attitude and the advantages of "defecting." They do not, and will not, always succeed.

That we have as strong a tendency as we do to act content-consistently instead of rationalizing is a contingent fact that depends on the balance of selective pressures. Some factors favour it, and others oppose it. Natural selection for a particular feature does not always result in the development of an adaptation. The balance in this case ensures that reflexive rationalization will remain fairly common but that it will not supplant content-consistent behaviour in every case in which that behaviour is contrary to the interest of the agent. There is no reason to think that the balance will ever alter in such a way that the advantages of reflexive rationalization would always outweigh the advantages of content-consistent behaviour. There is, consequently, no reason to think that reflexive rationalization would replace content-consistent behaviour in every case in which it conflicted with the interest of the agent. Worries about the evolutionary elimination of morality would legitimately arise if and only if natural selection strongly favoured reflexive rationalization over content-consistent acts when the acts were not in our interests. Since there are inevitable limits to the biological value of reflexive rationalization, however, we are, as a species, biologically bound to be moral.

CULTURAL VARIATION WITH RESPECT TO MORAL NORMS

Different societies differ about what is right, and there are disagreements among people within the same society. Modern industrial societies abhor slavery, but there have been many in which it has been accepted. Evolutionary intuitionism has to explain how the variation in moral opinion is compatible with there being a single, invariable basis of morality. It has to explain the fallibility of moral intuitions.

Particular groups may develop norms that mandate content-inconsistent actions. Six factors help to explain the phenomenon. First, foundational attitudes are not the only relevant propositional attitudes. Beliefs about the antecedents, the intrinsic nature, and the consequences of acts are also determinants of intuitions. It is easy to get many of these other relevant beliefs wrong: ignorance and error are highly probable.

Many factors make us ignorant or lead us into error. We are not always in a position to acquire all the relevant information. We are not always willing or able to expend the effort required to get at the truth. We do not always explore the implications of our beliefs thoroughly enough. And we may be inclined to accept certain sorts of views more than others because of our way of life. False propositions can appear plausible, and we can often acquire considerable evidence, or what we take to be evidence, for them. As mentioned earlier, our memories are mutable. We naturally revise and edit them and can end up with false beliefs instead of true ones as a result. For instance, what memory researchers call "change bias" can lead us to think that a self-improvement program was more successful than it actually was.[7] We are naturally prone to commit certain kinds of errors – we have cognitive biases. For instance, we are more likely to come up with complex, ad hoc theoretical "explanations" for apparent falsifications of theories to which we are committed than we are to reject the theories.[8] We have a tendency to stop too soon when we are looking for explanations. Doctrines about the nature of the world and the nature of humanity, particularly religious ones, can lead us astray as well. Finally, we can confuse the dispositions produced by group selection, kin selection, and reciprocal altruism with the moral inclinations our foundational attitudes give us. If the former conflict with the latter, we can err with respect to our moral obligations.

Second, foundational attitudes are not introspectible and moral facts do not make themselves precisely and unambiguously known to us. As we shall see in the next chapter, our intuitive knowledge of morality is like our intuitive knowledge that we ought to use a sentence in the passive voice in a particular situation. We may be intuitively aware that we should, but we almost certainly will not be intuitively aware of why we should. Just as we can have false notions about why we should use sentences in the passive voice, we can have false notions about why something is morally right or wrong. In other words, as well as having mistaken beliefs about non-moral factors, people can have mistaken theories of morality, which may lead them astray.

Third, as we have seen, we may engage in reflexive rationalization. Mistaken beliefs often lead to objectively wrongful actions, and once people have committed those acts, the mistaken beliefs will be cemented psychologically through reflexive rationalization. Thus, reflexive rationalization can secure and perpetuate moral error. Moral "fossils" can make it very difficult to correct a situation. So far, I have spoken as though reflexive rationalization were a matter of attempting to excuse or justify deviation from objective morality, which is what would happen if a society's moral code accurately reflected the moral facts. However, reflexive rationalization can also solidify people's commitment to the moral code of their society. People can rationalize acts that are performed out of a desire to conform to an erroneous morality as well as a desire to pursue their own interests. For instance, lovers might rationalize a norm that requires premarital chastity by appealing to the commands of God and might also rationalize their failure to observe it by saying that they intend to marry. Once committed to a norm, people will use reflexive rationalization to "justify" deviating (out of self-interest) from it. Reflexive rationalization can both support a deviant consensus about the nature of right and wrong and enable individuals to violate norms they accept in order to further their own interests.

Fourth, some of the factors that make reflexive rationalization unprofitable operate only within societies in which people interact with one another. If anyone attempts to rationalize his deviation from the collective norms, others will tend to criticize, correct, or punish him. In contrast, a group that rationalizes collectively is far less likely to be criticized, corrected, or punished. If it is largely independent of other groups, there will be no motive for seeking agreement with them; what criticism there is can be dismissed, or there may be no criticism at all. Indeed, people may be motivated to exaggerate differences in order to disparage alien societies. This tactic could be advantageous if, for instance, there was competition for resources. Because the inferior or the wicked would be less likely to have a legitimate moral claim to them, it would be easier to deprive them of them. In short, there are pressures for conformity on members of societies that have little or no effect on the societies themselves.

Fifth, getting morality wrong will not affect the capacity of anyone's foundational attitude to improve his ability to plan, carry out, and preserve the fruits of projects that are in his long-term interest. After all, morality is a mere by-product. Moreover, getting morality wrong will not affect co-operation as long as every member of the co-operating group gets it wrong in the same way. Foundational attitudes by themselves do not constitute an insurmountable obstacle to getting morality wrong.

Sixth, there are powerful motives for conforming to the norms of one's society. For the group, since the goal is co-operation on long-term projects, moral unanimity is more important than being objectively right about moral matters. As just mentioned, getting morality wrong will not affect co-operation as long as everyone makes the same error. For the individual, conformity with his society's moral code is usually far more important than conformity with moral reality.

He wants to gain the benefits of co-operation, and adherence to the norms of his society reveals him as a reliable potential co-operator.

Given the factors listed, deviant norms would develop quite readily. Members of a small-scale society, for instance, would almost certainly have some relevant false beliefs and lack some relevant true ones. It would be statistically inevitable that some members would violate their objective moral obligations and then rationalize their actions. They might even develop theories on which their actions were counted as right or good and strongly resist the idea that they had done anything wrong. Others would tend to conform to the rationalizers' opinions in order to maintain their status as reliable co-operators. After all, since they had been rationalized, the wrongdoers' opinions would be more strongly held, and it would often be easier for others to conform than to dispute matters. Social pressure would spread the deviant norm and reinforce conformity among the members of the society, as would the denigration of outsiders. And the moral facts themselves would be no great obstacle to the distortion, although there would be a tendency for societies to "regress to the mean," because the most committed rationalizers would die off and their influence decline. The same sort of process would occur repeatedly. Consequently, it is highly improbable that the moral code of the society would reflect moral reality accurately. The same sorts of things would happen in every society and in subcultures within a complex society as well, albeit probably not to the same extent. Therefore, the variation in moral codes that we actually observe is what we should expect to see.

THE POSSIBILITY OF MORAL REFORMERS

It is possible for moral reformers to play a role. Because our actions are consistent or inconsistent with our foundational attitudes, there is a normative, as well as an empirical, aspect to evolutionary intuitionism. While the empirical aspect tells us that there will be variation in moral opinions, the normative aspect tells us that at most one of a set of divergent moral opinions will be correct. For example, while the empirical aspect tells us that societies will frequently rationalize inequalities, the normative aspect mandates a basic moral equality among all possessors and potential possessors of foundational attitudes. Biology generally inclines us towards partiality, but morality, despite its biological origin, requires that we be impartial. This conflict is possible on an evolutionary account of morality when morality is a by-product that is inseparable from an adaptation, as it is on my theory.

Evolutionary intuitionism implies that our natural moral instincts will tend to conform to moral reality. People have to be socialized into accepting the moral code of their society, which may not conform to their instincts. Although socialization takes time and effort, the process will be successful in most cases. However, there is no guarantee that it will be successful in all. When it is not successful, moral reformers may emerge: people whose natural moral instincts have not been perverted by socialization.

The false moral judgments of a society can puzzle people who have not been successfully socialized. If someone thinks that it is forbidden for him to perform an act when it is in fact obligatory, there will be a conflict between what his socially acceptable moral judgment tells him he should do and what his extended foundational attitude inclines him to do. Imagine someone who thinks he should be a utilitarian, who knows that using an innocent person as a scapegoat would prevent civil disorder, who infers that he ought to use the person as a scapegoat, but who nevertheless cannot bring himself to do so. His theory may tell him that it is right while his instincts tell him that it is wrong.

It is more probable that morally sensitive individuals will have the sense that something is wrong with their society's norms if they have not cemented their commitment to them through reflexive rationalization after acting in accordance with them. The less a person has rationalized adherence to socially accepted norms, the weaker will be his commitment. The weaker his commitment is, the more probable it is that his foundational attitude will be the deciding influence on his moral beliefs. He will have an intuition that his society's norms are mistaken and an impulse to act against them. Under the right conditions, such people can promote moral reform.

Potential moral reformers of the sort hypothesized help prevent a society's false moral ideology from permanently and universally supplanting the influence of our foundational attitudes. Typically, the reform will take time, with younger people being more likely to support it and older people more likely to object to or resist it, probably because older people are more likely to have acted in accordance with the old code and to have rationalized their conformity with it.

Reform will be more likely under certain conditions. For instance, it will be more likely when two different societies interact in significant and widespread positive ways on a more or less equal basis. The interacting groups will have to develop a common ethic in order to interact successfully, and there will be challenges to moral beliefs that would not have occurred if the societies had remained isolated. The interaction must be positive and the societies on an equal basis because, otherwise, it will just be a case of one society imposing its views on another – convergence is not the same thing as reform. Reform is also more probable when a society is undergoing other changes, such as changes in the primary modes of production, because a new economic system requires new rules, and if some rules are changing, others are liable to be questioned as well. Third, reform is more probable when the losers under an existing arrangement *demand* better treatment. For instance, a hierarchical social arrangement is unlikely to change in a more egalitarian direction through mere theorizing, or from the top down. The theoretical rationalization for the social arrangement must be challenged, but the arrangement must be challenged practically as well. Otherwise, the material gains of oppressors will tend to trump any theoretical qualms they may have, and the rationalization will remain intact and in place.

Societies can differ in how far they diverge from the ideal moral code that is mandated by the moral facts. The institutions of some societies may combat collective reflexive rationalization, institutions such as universities in which academics are free to analyse and criticize their own society. Some societies can be less ignorant and less in error than others. The more the influence of these factors is reduced and combated, the closer to the ideal a society's moral code is likely to be. The egalitarianism of cultural relativism is pernicious as well as false.

If the moral norms posited by evolutionary intuitionism more closely resemble the norms of societies in which the relevant negative influences are combated, that resemblance itself counts in favour of evolutionary intuitionism. However, it does not follow that the moral code of an advanced industrial democracy with highly developed educational and judicial systems is without qualification better than the code of a hunting and gathering society, say, and it does not follow that the latter group should adopt the moral code of the former. What minimizes loss of what we are committed to take be of value* also depends on objective differences in circumstances, which can justify differences in moral codes. While the ends of morality remain the same, the ways in which it is possible or reasonable to achieve the ends can vary with the situation. For instance, in a hunter/gatherer society, it would almost certainly be a moral disaster to substitute the sorts of private property rights of contemporary industrialized societies for the obligation to share with others. The reverse is also the case. An obligation to share would subvert and destroy a market economy.

I am not saying that there is such a thing as inevitable and irreversible progress in moral matters. People may be attracted to ideologies that cause a resurgence of error, perhaps fostered by false prophets. Making progress is hard work, and it is always necessary to defend moral gains, because the kinds of influences that led us astray in the first place may reassert themselves.

THE RATIONALITY OF MORAL HEROISM

Although many people escape the influence of their foundational attitudes through reflexive rationalization, not everyone is equally adept at it. There is probably natural variation in the capacity for rationalization. On one end of the continuum, there will be people with weak foundational attitudes who are readily socialized and who find what they consider good excuses very readily indeed. On the other will be people who are unable to rationalize either their own transgressions or the transgressions of their society. It will be difficult or impossible for society to socialize them into accepting a deviant moral code, and they will find it difficult or impossible to violate their own moral convictions. They may or may not be reformers. What I am going to argue here is that it is rational for such people to do what moral heroes do.

Three senses of the term "rationality" are important here. In one sense, it is rational to do what is to one's material advantage: call this "economic rationality." In a different sense, it is rational for an agent to avoid the disability that results from holding inconsistent propositions: call this "functional rationality." In other words, it is rational for an organism to do what keeps it functioning well and to avoid doing what would impair its functioning. The third sense of the term is "all-things-considered" rationality, which balances economic and functional rationality.

Someone with a desire-dependent extended foundational attitude who has no abnormally strong desires, who has little or no capacity to rationalize, and who has the option of acting in desire-compatible ways may actually find it impossible not to help another in need in most cases. Moreover, in line with the motivational superfluity of true moral judgments, he might do so without reflection or calculation. So, at one extreme, we should find people who closely resemble the Ukrainians who risked their lives to rescue Jews from the Nazis, people who find it almost impossible not to do that sort of thing, at least if they believe they can get away with it.

It would be irrational for this kind of person to try to do anything but to act in accordance with his foundational attitude. Attempting to do otherwise would impair his ability to carry out projects that were in his long-term interest. Doing otherwise and believing truly about his actions would render him inconsistent and capable only of acting in those ways that are consistent with both his foundational attitude and its negation. He might experience considerable debilitating psychological distress as a result of cognitive dissonance if he tried, and it might be literally impossible for him anyway. Natural variation could result in there being individuals who lack the capacity even to try to act content-inconsistently. In sum, for such people, some ways of achieving some ends, or avoiding some acts, would be unavailable. It would be functionally rational for them to act in ways that are content-consistent but economically irrational. Moreover, it would be rational all things considered, because for them the importance of acting in functionally rational ways would outweigh the importance of the gains that are contingent on acting in economically rational ways. Such cases are analogous to ones in which it is rational for someone to give up a high-paying job for the sake of his health. Moral heroes can be rational to act as unselfishly as they do even when rationality is cashed out in terms of self-interest.

It should now be clear that evolutionary intuitionism can explain the Good Samaritan observations. Good Samaritans are Good Samaritans because in most cases they can do nothing when confronted with human desperation but try to alleviate or eliminate it. Others approve of their actions because they are aware that Good Samaritans are doing something good: it is always good to preserve the valuable*. And, finally, Good Samaritans are regarded as especially virtuous just because they are especially virtuous. Unlike most of us, they are not prone to weakness of the will, and they do not engage in reflexive rationalization out of self-interest. They are admirable specimens of humanity.

For moral heroes, acting morally is rational, not because there is an extrinsic pay-off, but because it is in their nature to act morally. The moral of the story of the ring of Gyges in the *Republic* is that without external constraints, people would wickedly advance their own interests and satisfy their desires at the expense of others. But even those who succumbed to temptation would, at the very least, have to rationalize their crimes reflexively. Potential moral heroes who do not suffer from *akrasia* and who do not have much capacity to rationalize reflexively would commit none. They do not have the capacity to do otherwise than to act righteously. The rest of us do. However, people who do not have the natural potential to be moral heroes can attempt to emulate them by becoming aware of their tendency to rationalize reflexively and taking steps to counter it. Moreover, they have an obligation to try.

CONCLUSION

Neither the occurrence of wrongdoing nor the existence of variation in moral opinion shows that the moral facts hypothesized by evolutionary intuitionism do not exist. Since morality is the by-product of an adaptation, from the perspective of the individual organism it is almost always a cost and never a benefit to act morally. With a few exceptions, we should expect people to try to avoid fulfilling their obligations if they can do anything about it without incurring too great a cost. Reflexive rationalization will enable them to do so. The criticism of other people keeps individuals within groups in line but does not have the same effect on groups themselves. If groups deviate significantly from the norms that are an accurate reflection of the moral facts, most people will conform to the norms of the group and rationalize departing from those norms. But a few will be independent thinkers with the potential to become moral reformers. Given the weakness of the influence of foundational attitudes and the multiplicity of other factors, we should expect significant moral variation among cultures and within particular cultures over time, even though the foundation of human morality remains the same. The variation does not prove that evolutionary intuitionism is false any more than wrongdoing does.

6

The Meta-Ethics of Evolutionary Intuitionism

INTRODUCTION

Evolutionary intuitionism identifies as moral facts various relations between acts and desire-dependent extended foundational attitudes. In this chapter, I will show that there are uncontroversial facts of the same sort. In other words, I will "domesticate" the hypothesized moral facts by showing that I am not introducing a novel kind of thing for the sake of the theory. After that, I will argue that the is/ought gap is irrelevant to evolutionary intuitionism. It exists, but it is unnecessary to cross it. Like other stock objections to adaptationist evolutionary ethics, the objection that evolutionary ethics involves deriving prescriptions from descriptions is not transferable. Since I am advancing a form of ethical intuitionism, I will explain the nature of the moral intuitions that evolutionary intuitionism gives us. I will show that evolutionary intuitionism escapes the fate of most versions of intuitionism by demonstrating that we do not have to rely on intuitions to reach normative conclusions and that we can corroborate some of them. It follows that cognitivism is true. Realism and objectivism are also true. Moreover, the same morality is universal among human societies, and it is not necessarily relative to species.

THE ORDINARINESS OF MORAL FACTS

If moral facts are constituted by the relations between acts and foundational attitudes, then they are not a unique kind of fact. They are like the fact that a set of propositions is inconsistent or like the fact that a person is hypocritical. Moreover, the relation of true moral beliefs to moral facts is similar to the relation between a true belief about inconsistency to the fact of inconsistency or the relation of a true belief about hypocrisy to the fact of hypocrisy.

Given evolutionary intuitionism, the fact that someone has done wrong is constituted by a relationship between his act and his foundational attitude. A true belief that someone is a wrongdoer is about the relationship between his act and his foundational attitude. The belief is true in virtue of the relationship. We do not logically derive the conclusion that he is a wrongdoer from his foundational attitude. Instead, we perceive a contradiction and judge that he is a wrongdoer in light of the fact that he is inconsistent.

Cases of wrongdoing closely resemble cases involving inconsistent sets of propositions. First, a belief about the inconsistency of the set is true in virtue of the relations between the members of the set. Similarly, a true moral belief is true in virtue of the relation between a foundational attitude and the true descriptions of an act. Second, a true belief about the set can be true even though some or all members of the set of propositions are false. Similarly, a moral belief can be true even if foundational attitudes are false. Third, the belief about the set is not logically derived from the propositions that are members of the set. Similarly, moral beliefs are not logically derived from a foundational attitude and a true description of the act that the moral belief is about. Fourth, we prove that a set is inconsistent by deriving a contradiction from the members of the set. Similarly, we prove that an act is wrong by showing that its true descriptions are inconsistent with foundational attitudes. Finally, there is no doubt about the existence of the relations between the members of a set of propositions in virtue of which the set is consistent or inconsistent, regardless of whether the members of the set are true or false. Similarly, if there are foundational attitudes, there is no doubt that they can stand in a variety of relations with acts, even though they are false.

Note also the similarities with cases of hypocrisy. For instance, someone might declare falsely that he should not favour his own offspring over other children and yet show the normal preference for his own. It would be a fact that he is a hypocrite; his being hypocritical would depend on the relation between his stated moral beliefs and his acts. He would be hypocritical even if the relevant moral belief was false. The fact that someone is hypocritical is constituted by the relevant relation between his stated beliefs and his acts. The true belief that someone is a hypocrite is a belief about the relationship between his stated beliefs and his acts. It is true because the appropriate relation exists. We do not logically derive the conclusion that he is hypocritical from his beliefs. We note a contradiction and judge that he is a hypocrite in light of the fact that he is inconsistent.

Moral facts are not like facts about hypocrisy in all respects, however. One can avoid being a hypocrite either by acting in accordance with one's stated beliefs or by giving them up. One does not, however, have two ways of avoiding wrongdoing, because one cannot avoid adopting a foundational attitude in the first place and one cannot discard it. Our foundational attitudes are permanent and resilient. Becoming amoral in order to maintain consistency is not an option. Consequently, the only way to avoid deserving moral disapprobation is to avoid performing the relevant acts.

To contend that the moral properties of acts are constituted by the relations between the acts and foundational attitudes should be no more controversial than, say, to claim that the moral properties of acts are reducible to the properties of decreasing or increasing the total amount of preference satisfaction. The latter reduction is uncontroversial not because it is widely accepted as giving the right account of morality but because it is accepted as a plausible candidate for being the right account of morality. Similarly, there is nothing inherently implausible about moral properties being relations between acts and foundational attitudes or about there being moral beliefs that are true in virtue of corresponding to the relations.

The fact that a set of propositions is logically consistent is ordinary and unremarkable. Since it is unproblematic, there is no reason why moral facts constituted by the relations between acts and foundational attitudes should be questionable. J.L. Mackie contends that it is improbable that there are moral facts that exist independently of human beings and their cultures because such moral facts would be entirely unlike any other facts of which we are aware. "If there were objective values, then they would be entities or qualities or relations of a very strange sort, utterly different from anything else in the universe."[1] Mackie's objection does not adversely affect my account of moral facts, however, because the moral facts evolutionary intuitionism posits are not "utterly different from anything else in the universe."

THE IRRELEVANCE OF THE IS/OUGHT GAP

David Hume pointed out the invalidity of moving from purely descriptive premises to a normative conclusion.[2] Elliott Sober summarizes Hume's point as follows: "Hume's thesis says that *a deductively valid argument for an ought-conclusion must have at least one ought-premiss.*"[3] Sober argues for a non-deductive counterpart to Hume's thesis. "*Purely is-premisses cannot, by themselves, provide non-deductive support for an ought-conclusion.*"[4] Both Hume's thesis and Sober's non-deductive counterpart seem right, and neither is a problem for evolutionary intuitionism. True moral judgments are not inferred either from foundational attitudes or from the moral facts that are constituted by the relations between acts and foundational attitudes.

As for true moral judgments being inferred from foundational attitudes, since foundational attitudes are false, there is no reliable way to derive true moral judgments from them using truth-preserving rules of inference, and there are no sound deductive arguments with them as premises. Moreover, also since they are false, foundational attitudes cannot provide non-deductive support for true moral judgments. Since moral judgments are not inferred from foundational attitudes, there can be true moral judgments even though foundational attitudes are false. The falsity of foundational attitudes does not infect moral judgments any more than the falsity of a member of a set of propositions infects claims about the set's consistency or inconsistency.

Foundational attitudes are not moral principles. A moral principle is a generalization from which it is possible to derive particular moral judgments provided that it is coupled with relevant, true descriptions of acts. In other words, a moral principle can function as a premise in an argument. Foundational attitudes cannot function in the same way. Instead, they participate in various relations with acts, the relations constitute moral facts, and moral beliefs are about the relations. If foundational attitudes were moral principles, there would be no moral facts. At best, there would be beliefs about right and wrong. Evolutionary intuitionism holds that there are moral facts, not merely that we believe there are.

True moral judgments are not inferred from moral facts constituted by the relations between acts and foundational attitudes; it is not a matter of inference at all. Imagine that there is a cat on the mat in front of the stove in the kitchen on a cold windy day. Consider two people, the cat's owner and a first-time visitor. The cat's owner knows that the cat exists, knows that it has a predilection for sleeping on the mat in front of the stove on cold windy days, and knows that it is a cold windy day. The first-time visitor knows nothing about the cat's habits. The cat's owner is not looking toward the stove. The visitor is. Now, suppose that both believe that the cat is on the mat. The owner believes it because he infers that the cat is on the mat. The visitor believes it because he apprehends that state of affairs. But the two modes of belief acquisition are fundamentally different. The owner's belief and the reasons for it could be, respectively, the conclusion and the premises of an argument. The visitor's belief and the reasons for it could not.

Inference is an intellectual movement from proposition to proposition. Apprehension is the acquisition of a belief in response to a state of affairs. Our ability to apprehend states of affairs is not fundamentally an ability to make inferences, no matter what sorts of inferences. It is an ability to see that such and such is the case. With evolutionary intuitionism, we intuitively apprehend the fact, say, that torture is wrong. We do not infer the belief that torture is wrong from other propositions. Since inference is not involved, the impossibility of inferring an "ought" from an "is" is not relevant. The is/ought gap is of no significance whatsoever for evolutionary intuitionism.

INTROSPECTION AND INTUITION

Evolutionary intuitionism can explain our intuitive access to the hypothesized moral facts. Our intuition on my theory is not the same as the moral sense – not as Darwin thought of it at any rate. For Darwin, the moral sense is not a faculty for sensing moral truths but the sensation of there being moral truths.[5] For Darwin, the moral sense is constituted by beliefs about what is right and wrong. He provides a causal explanation for our moral beliefs in terms of sympathy, memory, language, and habit. We end up believing that there are moral facts, but we do not end up believing that there are moral facts because we have apprehended them. The topic here is how we intuitively apprehend moral facts. It is not how moral beliefs come into existence.

It may seem implausible that there are foundational attitudes, because no one is aware of them; no one introspects them. It may appear that they might as well not be there at all. But the notion that all propositional attitudes are introspectible and that only introspectible propositional attitudes can influence behaviour is false. A human being cannot show that he lacks a foundational attitude by inspecting the conscious contents of his mind and noting its apparent absence.[6]

The air of implausibility here can be reduced by showing that there are beliefs that we cannot introspect. Here is one example. Grammarians sometimes posit beliefs that cannot be introspected in order to explain linguistic phenomena. For instance, native speakers of standard English use the active voice on some occasions and the passive voice on others. In almost all cases, a sentence conveys the same information in either voice. In many cases, the reason one or the other is used is that the speaker is obeying the principle of end-focus, which is that information unknown to the audience should go at the end of the sentence. If someone knows how to speak standard English, then he tends to place information at the end of sentences whenever he *believes* that it is unknown to his listeners, provided that he has the grammatical resources to do so and provided that there is no more important consideration to attend to.[7] If his belief is false, then he will use an inappropriate form. But speakers of standard English do not introspect the beliefs about the knowledge of their audience that govern their linguistic behaviour, as is evident from the widespread occurrence of incorrect explanations for the use of the passive voice, when any explanation is given at all.

Having "domesticated" some beliefs that are out of introspective range, I am now in a position to do the same with respect to intuitions, using the same example. In the same way that the moral facts hypothesized are not the only ones of their kind, the way in which we can apprehend moral facts is not unique either. If there are foundational attitudes, moral intuitions are analogous to our linguistic intuitions concerning the use of the active and passive voices in standard English. Language-users are commonly able to say that a particular construction is correct, or preferable, in a particular case without being able to say why. Most native speakers of standard English are able to say that the passive is preferable to the active in cases in which the explanation has to do with the principle of end-focus and their beliefs about the knowledge of the audience. At the same time, they are unable to explain why it is preferable. They just have linguistic *intuitions* about what is correct, intuitions that are a function of what they believe, even though they cannot introspect the relevant beliefs.

Bernard Williams objects that the analogy between linguistic and moral intuitions is weak.[8] He says that differences in linguistic intuitions can be explained by referring to the speakers' dialects and that we do not need to refer to linguistic theory to explain them, whereas we do need to refer to theory to sort out moral intuitions. His objection has no force here, however, since I am talking about the speakers of a single dialect, standard English, and about only some of their linguistic intuitions, ones they all share.

It probably works this way. If someone tends to obey the principle of end-focus and if using the passive voice enables him to put new information at the end, not putting new information at the end would be inconsistent with the information being new. If he believes that some information is new, then he tends to act consistently with its being new and inconsistently with its being old. (There is no reason to think that this tendency is connected with conscious belief only.) In those circumstances, he would experience an impulse to put the information believed to be new at the end, feeling that a sentence in which it was at the beginning was awkward. Even if he were unable to explain why, he would have an *intuition* that he ought to do the grammatically correct thing.

The moral intuitions of people with foundational attitudes are like these particular linguistic intuitions of native speakers of standard English. Possessors are able to say what is morally right without being able to say why. They possess attitudes that they cannot introspect but that influence their inclinations and whose influence they notice. Foundational attitudes are part of the cause of moral intuitions in the same way that beliefs about what our audience knows are part of the cause of some linguistic intuitions.

If evolutionary intuitionism is true, we had moral intuitions as soon as we acquired foundational attitudes and the relations between acts and foundational attitudes came into existence, because our moral intuitions are caused by our foundational attitudes and their relations to our acts. Our access to the moral facts is as direct as our access to our own bodily aches and pains, although moral facts are more ambiguous and more liable to misinterpretation. They are ambiguous and liable to misinterpretation because we can misunderstand the nature of the world and our own acts. When there is no misunderstanding, our intuitions reflect the moral facts without distortion. If evolutionary intuitionism is true, then under ideal conditions our intuitions and the implications of evolutionary intuitionism ought to agree. As mentioned in chapter 4, it follows that substantial intuitive failure would falsify the theory, not because intuitive acceptability is a universal standard that all theories must try to meet, but because we can predict the agreement because of the causal relationship between moral facts and moral intuitions.

The ability to articulate and express our moral intuitions no doubt took some time. It would have been necessary to invent new terms for our new experiences or to learn to use old terms in new ways. Our terminology tells us nothing about moral reality itself, however. At most, it may reveal something about our moral theories.

The second part of Mackie's argument about the strangeness of objective moral facts is that if they did exist independently of us, our awareness of them would be mysterious: "if we were aware of them, it would have to be by some special faculty of moral perception or intuition, utterly different from our ordinary ways of knowing everything else."[9] However, the way in which we become aware of moral facts is as ordinary as the facts themselves. There can be no reasonable doubt that linguistic intuitions are a source of linguistic knowledge. Our utterances and inscriptions often contain errors, and we must rely on linguistic intuitions to sort them out. Some linguistic intuitions tell us what is correct or preferable when that depends on what we believe and when we are unable to introspect the relevant beliefs. Moral intuitions are as ordinary as linguistic intuitions.

THE CORROBORATION OF MORAL INTUITIONS

Ethical intuitionism is widely rejected. Most versions of it are flawed because they are not accompanied by an independent criterion that we can apply to distinguish reliable intuitions from unreliable ones. As a result, not only do they allow a lot of armchair pontification but they also permit multiple pontificators. Each could contradict the others, and we would have no way of discovering which, if any of them, was right. Evolutionary intuitionism is not flawed in this way, because moral intuitions are superfluous for moral theorizing and discovering what is right and wrong. The moral status of acts can be determined by discovering whether they are consistent with the foundational attitudes of the relevant agents. We can determine whether foundational attitudes exist through empirical investigation. And we can use deductive logic to determine whether acts are consistent with them. Consequently, evolutionary intuitionism does not require us, in principle, to *rely* on intuitions for any of our normative conclusions. We can, in principle, determine the moral facts in another way. True moral judgments are those that correspond to moral facts. Therefore, evolutionary intuitionism avoids the flaw that vitiates other versions of ethical intuitionism. We can corroborate some of our moral intuitions independently; we have moral intuitions, but we also have an alternative to accessing moral reality by means of them.

If some moral beliefs are true and if it is possible to establish that they are true, then there can be justified moral beliefs. They are obviously justified when we have grounds to believe that they correspond to the moral facts. Consequently, if evolutionary intuitionism is justified and if it enables us to determine the moral facts, then some possible moral judgments could be justified. However, I want to resist the grandiose conclusion that we have, in the light of evolutionary intuitionism, finally gained moral knowledge. So, I will show that it has always been possible for us to have moral knowledge if reliabilism is true. Reliabilism is the theory of knowledge that claims that we have knowledge when we reliably apprehend states of affairs even if we do not know that we reliably apprehend them.[10]

Evolutionary intuitionism entails that human beings are reliable detectors of moral facts under certain conditions, namely, when a person possesses all relevant true beliefs but no relevant false beliefs and when he is unbiased and disinterested. If he is ignorant or has mistaken beliefs, his intuitions will not really be about the state of affairs he is purportedly judging. It is obvious why he must be unbiased and disinterested. But he must be unbiased and disinterested not merely with respect to the moral belief token about which he is to judge but also about the moral belief type, or even about a range of similar moral belief types. Someone is unbiased and disinterested with respect to a moral belief type when he has not rationalized reflexively in connection with a relevantly similar case. His previous reflexive rationalization in the same type of case might skew his judgment in the present case. The reason why a knowledgeable, unbiased, and disinterested person would be a competent moral judge is that the main reasons for variation in moral intuitions are ignorance, error, and reflexive rationalization. If one such person makes a moral judgment, we have good evidence that the judgment is true. If several such judges do so independently and if they concur, the evidence verges on the conclusive. So, if reliabilism is true and if evolutionary intuitionism is true, then we can possess moral knowledge even if we cannot demonstrate that we do. We can have moral knowledge even if we cannot refute the sceptic. If reliabilism is true, it has always been possible for us to have moral knowledge. Moreover, it has always been possible for us to be intuitively aware of this state of affairs; we could always suspect that there is such a thing as moral knowledge.

THE IMPOSSIBILITY OF MORAL PRINCIPLES

Evolutionary intuitionism justifies our reliance on moral intuitions. If the theory is true, then foundational attitudes are part of the causal explanation for our intuitions. Therefore, it would be odd if the intuitions of knowledgeable, unbiased, and disinterested people and the results of the theory were substantially in conflict. Unfortunately, since the ideal is rarely achieved, we cannot depend uncritically or absolutely on our intuitions. However, we cannot compensate merely by trying to achieve coherence. Evolutionary intuitionism is a foundationalist doctrine; what matters is the relation of moral judgments to moral facts. A coherentist approach, on which the relations of intuitive moral judgments to each other are paramount, could lead us astray, as I will argue in this section.

The standard procedure of many philosophers who do normative ethics is to try to devise a self-consistent moral principle from which, in conjunction with relevant, true descriptions of acts, it is possible to derive all and only true moral judgments. In other words, the standard procedure is to attempt to impose principle-centred consistency. I have not tried, and will not try, to show that any moral principle is true. It is not just that principles are superfluous (because we can discover what the moral facts are in another way and there is an alternative way of reasoning about moral matters) but that they are impossible. Foundational attitudes are desire-dependent, and to accommodate their desire-dependence, principles would have to include provisos of the form "except when conditions c_1 or … or c_n obtain." Principles with this kind of exception clause would be too accommodating. It would be possible to "justify" any principle whatsoever. Of course, when there is a system of principles that can conflict in practice, there can be exceptions to some principles when they are outranked or outweighed by other principles. Moreover, it need not be the case that the rankings are constant no matter what the circumstances. But provisos of the form "except when conditions c_1 or ... or c_n obtain" would pick out exceptions to the entire system of principles, not just some members of it on some occasions.

There is no justifiable equivalent that refers not to the relations between a foundational attitude and acts but to other properties of acts themselves, their consequences, or the antecedent dispositions of the agents. No principle like "It is obligatory to maximize preference satisfaction" is at all likely to work. Trying to concoct one would be like trying to define parenthood in terms of the properties of parents while excluding any reference to offspring. According to evolutionary intuitionism, moral properties are relational properties. They are not intrinsic properties of acts, properties of their antecedents, or properties of their consequences. Moreover, if any such principle enabled us to pick out all and only true moral judgments, it would be accidental that it did so. No one would be justified in endorsing it.

The principle "Minimize loss of value* unless ..." would not do, because value* is not actually instantiated. "Minimize loss of what you take to be of value* unless ..." would also not do because there are no restrictions on what people can take to be of value*. "Minimize loss of what you are committed to take to be of value* unless ..." would have to be glossed by a recapitulation of the entire theory. In fact, any good "principle" would be a restatement of the description of the structure of moral facts: "It is obligatory for you to act consistently with the proposition 'I am of value* and N^1 is of value* and ... and N^k is of value*' and inconsistently with its negation when you hold that you are of value* and when acting consistently with it is compatible with your desire to avoid significant injury being your strongest desire when you act, etc." Translating the description into this kind of "principle" falsifies it by transforming a description of the structure of moral facts, to which true moral judgments correspond, into a generalized moral judgment. Some moral judgments of the form "It is obligatory that ..." are true because they correspond to moral facts, but the facts cannot be their own moral justification, and there is no justification for their existence. Their existence is explicable in evolutionary terms, but evolutionary explanations do not constitute justifications.

The impossibility of moral principles forms the basis for an objection. Some commentators think that people naturally theorize like philosophers who try to impose principle-centred consistency on intuitions and that their utterances with respect to why acts are right or wrong are elliptical deductive justifications. Suppose that the efforts of philosophers are "*merely* more technical and more systematic."[11] We could then justifiably conclude that morality is not based on foundational attitudes.

There is another plausible interpretation of people's natural verbal behaviour, however. If one person tells another that some act is wrong and the latter asks why, the former may reply, for instance, that it would hurt a third party. This claim need not be a premise in a deductive argument with the appropriate conclusion. Instead, it could be a reminder about a relevant aspect of the situation. The questioner would thereby be enabled to see intuitively why the act was wrong, provided that he was rational and possessed a foundational attitude. The situation is analogous to one in which an English teacher notices that a student has used the present perfect tense in a sentence and reminds him that he has used the adverb "yesterday" as well. The teacher expects that he will understand that the tense needs to be changed from present perfect to simple past or that the adverb needs to be replaced by one that refers to a period of time that includes the present. Neither thinks that the use of the adverb is part of a deductive justification for using the simple past tense. Because teacher and student share the same language to some extent, the student realizes what he must do. Similarly, the answer to a question of why something is wrong could be a reminder to someone who speaks the same moral language – in other words, to someone who also has a foundational attitude.

REALISM, OBJECTIVITY, AND UNIVERSALITY

We have seen that evolutionary intuitionism is a cognitivist theory. It is also realist, objectivist, and universalist. To affirm moral realism is simply to affirm that there are moral facts. Whatever support there is for the existence of moral facts is also support for moral realism. Enough has already been said about the moral facts of evolutionary intuitionism to establish that it is a realist doctrine, but the issues of objectivity and universality cannot be dealt with quite so quickly.

I will argue in detail in this section that evolutionary intuitionism gives us an objective morality. There has been a debate over whether adaptationist evolutionary ethics can be objective. Some philosophers have argued that it cannot be objective;[12] others have argued that it can.[13] I am not interested in this debate. Objective or not, adaptationism cannot give a satisfactory account of the Good Samaritan observations discussed in chapter 1. My sole concern here will be to show that evolutionary intuitionism gives us an objective morality. After discussing the objective nature of morality (given evolutionary intuitionism), I will argue that not merely is morality the same in every human society but that it need not be limited to humanity.

If there are moral facts constituted by relations between acts and foundational attitudes, then morality is objective as well. In this context, Richmond Campbell's definition of "objective" will serve. Campbell "count[s] a justification for the existence of morals as objective if three conditions are met: (1) The justification is a fact in the same sense that the facts of evolution are taken to be facts; (2) the justification does not depend on anyone's moral beliefs; and (3) the justification is (within broad limits) insensitive to the specific content of the preferences and desires of those for whom the existence of morals is to be justified."[14] Evolutionary intuitionism is objective on Campbell's definition. There are moral facts, which are constituted by the relations between foundational attitudes and acts. They may not be facts in exactly the same sense that the facts of evolution are facts, but they are certainly close enough. The moral facts hypothesized do not depend on our moral beliefs. Indeed, our moral beliefs depend on their relationship to the facts for their truth-value, but the facts can exist without the beliefs. According to evolutionary intuitionism, true moral beliefs cannot exist without the facts. Finally, the moral facts postulated by evolutionary intuitionism are the same whatever we prefer or desire; our preferences and desires may accord with, conflict with, or be neutral with respect to the moral facts.

Evolutionary intuitionism enables us to convincingly rebut Mackie's case against objectivity in ethics, which he summarized as follows. "The considerations that favour moral scepticism are: first, the relativity or variability of some important starting points of moral thinking and their apparent dependence on actual ways of life; secondly, the metaphysical peculiarity of the supposed objective values, in that they would have to be intrinsically action-guiding and motivating; thirdly, the problem of how such values could be consequential or supervenient on natural features; fourthly, the corresponding epistemological difficulty ... fifthly, the possibility of explaining ... how even if there were no objective values people might not only have come to suppose that there are but also might persist firmly in that belief."[15]

Evolutionary intuitionism can respond satisfactorily to each of the points. As for the first, I argued in chapter 5 that evolutionary intuitionism enables us to predict that there will be variation in moral codes. Moreover, there is no mystery about why moral codes would be correlated with ways of life. The reasons for the variation in moral codes are also reasons for the correlation because of the importance of social co-operation. As for the second, I have argued in this chapter that moral facts are an ordinary sort of fact, and in the previous chapter I explained how they motivate us. As for the third, there is an adequate response in chapter 2. Moral facts are constituted by the relationship between acts and foundational attitudes. The relationship is not one of supervenience, but that does not matter. With respect to the fourth, I have explained how we can have moral knowledge in this chapter and argued that there are two ways in which we can acquire it.

Finally, contrary to Mackie, it is doubtful that there is an adequate anti-realist explanation for our belief in objective moral values. One "explanation" he provides is that the belief in objective ethics originates when we postulate a system of law and leave out the legislator. This is no more than a "just-so" story. Another is that it is the consequence of our projecting our "wants and demands"[16] onto the world. Supposedly, "we need morality to regulate interpersonal relations, to control some of the ways in which people behave towards one another, often in opposition to contrary inclinations. We therefore want our moral judgements to be authoritative for other agents as well as for ourselves: objective validity would give them the authority required."[17] The projection could be either an adaptation or a cultural innovation. As for the former, adaptationist evolutionary ethics was rejected in the first chapter. As for the latter, a purely cultural explanation faces a number of difficulties even if we ignore evolution. The fact that morality might further everyone's interests is far from enough to guarantee its development. It is necessary to do more than to describe a motive for inventing it. It is also necessary to show that people are insightful enough to find it attractive. It must be shown that the development of morality is achievable and that it would be stable once achieved. It must be established that humanity does not confront a prisoner's dilemma such that people end up acting contrary to their interests and failing to develop morality as a result. It will have to be explained why there appear to be well-socialized psychopaths, people who appear to understand the nature of morality but who do not endorse it. In other words, it must be explained why "objective validity" is authoritative for ordinary people but not for psychopaths. Mackie does not notice, let alone overcome, these difficulties. Even if they could be overcome, explaining objectivity away is attractive only when Mackie's first four contentions are not satisfactorily rebutted. Evolutionary intuitionism is an objectivist theory that refutes them. It vindicates objectivism.

Michael Ruse and Edward O. Wilson share Mackie's anti-realism. They claim that "human beings function better if they are deceived by their genes into thinking that there is a disinterested objective morality binding upon them, which all should obey."[18] They agree with Mackie that all our moral beliefs are false. There are no true moral beliefs because there are no facts to which they could possibly correspond. Ethics is the biological equivalent of the noble lie. In contrast, evolutionary intuitionism claims that evolution gives us moral facts constituted by foundational attitudes, which are products of variation and natural selection, and their relationships with acts. We acquire moral beliefs in response to the moral facts. Evolutionary intuitionism does not claim that moral beliefs are products of evolution but that there is an objective morality. It explains its origin and its nature. The evidence for evolutionary intuitionism and against adaptationism is evidence against evolutionary ethics as an error theory.

Like Mackie, Ruse and Wilson are relativists, but they are evolutionary, not cultural, relativists. They contend that "ethical premises are peculiar products of genetic history, and they can be understood solely as mechanisms that are adaptive for the species that possess them. It follows that the ethical code of one species cannot be translated into that of another. No abstract moral principles exist outside the particular nature of the species."[19]

In stark contrast, evolutionary intuitionism denies that moral codes can be understood solely as adaptive mechanisms. It holds that morality is not necessarily relative to the species and that, on the contrary, it is highly probable that non-human moral agents would share the same morality with human moral agents. The reasons for this are as follows.

First, moral facts are constituted by the relations between foundational attitudes and acts, which do not depend on anyone's moral beliefs, principles, theories, or perspectives or on their likes, desires, or preferences. It is an objective fact, if it is a fact, that a set of propositions is inconsistent. It is also an objective fact, if it is a fact, that someone has done wrong. If it were wrong for one person with a foundational attitude, it would be wrong for any possessor in similar circumstances, not because the moral properties of the acts supervene on the non-moral properties but because in relevantly similar circumstances, the respective acts of the agents each stand in the same relation to a foundational attitude. The acts are relevantly similar, the circumstances are relevantly similar, the foundational attitudes are propositions of the same form. The only difference is that the referents of the names, pronouns, or definite descriptions are different. In other words, the only difference is that numerically distinct possessors of foundational attitudes are involved.

Second, being a member of the human species is not a necessary condition for being a moral agent. Since the existence of human morality depends upon the existence of foundational attitudes, there are good evolutionary reasons to think that moral truths and moral facts are fundamentally the same for members of every human culture. This does not prevent variation in moral codes, however, as we saw in chapter 5. But it does not follow that being human is a necessary condition for being a moral agent. There is no reason to think that only human beings could have foundational attitudes. Daughter species of *Homo sapiens sapiens* could, and probably would, have them. Incidentally, being human is not a sufficient condition either. I have not argued that foundational attitudes have reached fixation, the situation in which every member of the species possesses one. If they have not, then some human beings will lack foundational attitudes. I believe that psychopaths lack them.

Finally, there is no reason to think that foundational attitudes could not evolve independently more than once. Birds and bats both have wings, but neither group of species is descended from the other, nor are they descended from the same winged ancestors. If foundational attitudes evolved more than once, it would be possible for human beings to share the same morality with members of other species even though they have not inherited foundational attitudes from a common ancestor. Moreover, perhaps only foundational attitudes could produce what an intuitionist would regard as morality. If so, foundational attitudes could be the cause of a species' having a morality in every case. There might be as close a connection between being a moral agent and possessing a foundational attitude as there is between being able to see and having eyes, which are known to have evolved more than once. Every foundational attitude has a biological origin but there is no reason to think that they must all have a common biological origin. The morality of evolutionary intuitionism can be shared by more than one species because more than one species can possess foundational attitudes. There would be selection for them because they are advantageous no matter the species' circumstances and no matter the species' history.

From an intuitionist perspective, which denies that sociality necessarily leads to morality, only human beings appear to be moral agents. But it is a contingent, not a necessary, truth. If we ever encounter an extraterrestrial species with a culture approximately as advanced as ours, we might find that they have foundational attitudes and that we share a common moral understanding. Unlike adaptationist evolutionary ethics, evolutionary intuitionism is not relativistic.

One final point can be added. As well as being objective and universal among human societies, moral truths are absolute in that there are no reasons that outweigh moral reasons. The desire-dependence of foundational attitudes so delimits the range of moral facts that there is no justification for permitting other reasons to outweigh moral ones. Desire-dependence is enough of a concession to our needs and our nature.

CONCLUSION

Evolutionary intuitionism hypothesizes a complex of adaptations resulting in desire-dependent extended foundational attitudes. It contends that the relations between acts and those attitudes constitute moral facts. Evolutionary intuitionism rehabilitates and vindicates intuitionism by giving a naturalistic account of intuitions that explains how we can successfully access moral facts. From an intuitionist perspective, the hypothesized moral facts explain our meta-ethical "observations." The word, "observations," is in scare quotes because meta-ethical views are liable to be controversial and theory-laden. However, the plausibility of the alternatives often depends on the supposed failure of realism, objectivism, and cognitivism, which have the status of default positions. I have not argued abstractly for the doctrines. Instead, I have argued for an explanation of human morality whose truth guarantees their truth. Meta-ethically, it is enough to justify reverting to the default positions.

7

Evaluating Evolutionary Intuitionism

INTRODUCTION

Evolutionary intuitionism is a theory about the foundations of human morality. If the arguments in the first chapter of this book are sound, it is the right kind of theory. The theory provides a testable evolutionary account of the origin of moral facts without explaining morality away. There are, literally, moral facts about what is permissible, what is obligatory, and what is forbidden. We do not just believe that there are: there is real moral normativity in the world, which derives from the normative concepts that are constituents of the contents of our foundational attitudes. The moral facts are neither unique nor strange. Their existence explains why certain meta-ethical and normative claims are true. Foundational attitudes motivate us to act morally. So how good is the theory as a theory?

EVOLUTIONARY INTUITIONISM AS A BY-PRODUCT THEORY

There was selection for desire-dependent extended foundational attitudes because they benefited the individual organism. There was selection for extended foundational attitudes because co-operation with other possessors benefited the individual. There was selection for desire-dependence because it benefited the individual by allowing him to reduce his exposure to potential harm in dangerous situations. Kin selection and reciprocal altruism contribute to morality only insofar as they produce the other forms of desire-dependence and, thus, limit potential obligations. It follows that if morality originated because of these developments, it must be a by-product rather than an adaptation. The reason is that some morally laudable acts are biologically altruistic, such as when they benefit strangers or other outsiders, and individual selection would tend to result in dispositions not to perform them. If morality were adaptive, then acts that benefit strangers would not be morally laudable. If morality is a by-product, however, there can be morally laudable acts that benefit strangers.

Evolutionary intuitionism does what a by-product evolutionary theory of human morality ought to do. Neven Sesardic claims that "to defend [by-product theories] one is under a threefold obligation: (i) to identify some other trait, (ii) to show that it was selected for, and (iii) to demonstrate that it is inextricably tied to [psychological altruism]."[1] To make Sesardic's observation relevant here, we merely have to replace "psychological altruism" with "morality." I have not done precisely what Sesardic recommends. I have posited another trait, foundational attitudes, and provided an evolutionary explanation for their origin. By identifying the relations between foundational attitudes and acts as moral facts, I have hypothesized an unseverable connection that enables us to predict the correlation between being a rationalizing moral agent and having the normal ability to carry out long-term projects. The correlation is evidence for the hypothetical arrangement as I have interpreted it.

THE INTUITIVE PLAUSIBILITY OF EVOLUTIONARY INTUITIONISM

What evolutionary intuitionism gives us in the way of normative conclusions is good enough to make it intuitively acceptable. It offers something both to our consequentialist and to our deontological intuitions. Sometimes, as the consequentialist believes, if some of a good thing is good, more is better. At other times, as the deontologist holds, nothing could be less plausible. Moreover, evolutionary intuitionism satisfies our consequentialist and deontological leanings on the right occasions. It is true that we should save as many lives as possible. It is not true that we should do it by sacrificing otherwise healthy and uninjured people. In addition, the distinction is not ad hoc but flows directly from the theory as a consequence of desire-dependence. Desire-dependence increases biological fitness. I have not introduced it merely to make evolutionary intuitionism more plausible as a moral theory.

The theory explains the nature of our moral intuitions, that is, our natural access to moral facts. All normative theories ultimately depend on intuitions. Philosophers reject candidate theories because they have counter-intuitive implications. The main alternative to permitting intuitions to falsify theories is to declare allegiance to a theory and to stick with it whatever its implications. But that is merely to allow one's initial intuitive judgment to outweigh all subsequent qualms. In contrast, because it explains how it is that moral truths are true, evolutionary intuitionism is freed from relying on intuitions. It explains moral intuitions; it does not depend on them.

Instead of relying on intuitions, evolutionary intuitionism transforms normative ethics into a field that can be investigated empirically. The fact that the theory is empirically testable refutes the view that observations are irrelevant to ethical inquiry. For example, it refutes Gilbert Harman's contention that "there does not seem to be observational evidence, even indirectly, for basic moral principles."[2] The empirical implications of evolutionary intuitionism have to do with moral facts rather than moral principles, but the difference is not important in this context. The theory shows that the normative and the empirical are not necessarily entirely separate and distinct. Although moral facts of the sort hypothesized unify the factual and the normative by showing how real moral facts can come into existence in a world previously devoid of them, Hume's is/ought gap is still there. We cannot infer normative truths from purely factual premises, either deductively or non-deductively.

The moral facts the theory gives us must correspond reasonably closely to our moral intuitions because foundational attitudes are part of the causal explanation for our intuitions. Thus, even as the theory frees us from reliance on intuitions when it comes to theorizing, it helps us justify reliance on them in practical matters. As mentioned in a previous chapter, there are distorting factors. When I say that the moral facts must correspond to our moral intuitions, I mean that they must correspond when distorting factors are absent.

THE VALUE OF THE EMPIRICAL EVIDENCE

Evolutionary intuitionism predicts universality, reflexive rationalization, and a positive correlation between being moral and being able to carry out long-term projects as well as we do. Most metaethical and normative moral theories are compatible with the three states of affairs, but we should adhere to a higher standard than that. Compatibility shows only that the theories are not falsified by observations but does not entail that the theory explains them.

Not all theories are likely to do as well as evolutionary intuitionism by explaining universality. If morality is the by-product of an adaptation with which it is inextricably connected, there is a well-understood type of causal explanation for its spread throughout the species. In contrast, preference satisfaction utilitarianism, for example, has difficulties with universality, since it holds that all preferences of all beings with preferences should be taken into consideration and is therefore confronted with the problem that human nature is a product of evolution. Concern for the satisfaction of all preferences would never become universal, because partiality is biologically preferable to impartiality. There are strong selection pressures for the elimination of impartiality. Of course, preference satisfaction utilitarians do not usually aim to explain universality; no doubt, they have not seen the need to do so. Nonetheless, they have an intellectual obligation to show that their theory is consistent with human nature.

Many theories would do worse than evolutionary intuitionism when it comes to explaining reflexive rationalization. Evolutionary intuitionism explains the phenomenon as the result of foundational attitudes being permanent and resilient and objective wrongdoing being advantageous and as the result of the high cost of holding beliefs that are inconsistent with one's foundational attitude. We cannot free ourselves from the grip of morality and if we violate our own moral code, we often have no alternative but to lie to ourselves about our own actions in order to maintain proper functioning. In contrast, if morality were the result of a social contract, say, there would seem to be no reason why a person could not simply reject the rules outright – in the same way some of those raised in the Church become irreligious. But people do not do so. Surely, however, if a person can free himself from some doctrines he has simply been socialized to hold, he ought to be able to free himself from others. The human preference for the rationalization of wrongful acts over the rejection of morality indicates that human beings cannot reject morality. Unlike other theories, evolutionary intuitionism explains why we cannot. Hence, reflexive rationalization provides strong support for evolutionary intuitionism. Other theories cannot necessarily appeal to it.

Not all theories predict a positive correlation between being a rationalizing moral agent and being a planner. Not all entail that there are no highly intelligent villains who can successfully carry out long-term evil designs without rationalizing reflexively about their actions. Not all entail that all true amoralists are incompetent when it comes to projects that are in their long-term interest. In fact, no other theory clearly does. It might appear that some others make the same prediction but the appearance is misleading. For instance, Thomas Nagel argues that our future interests constitute reasons to act now to advance those interests and that the interests of others stand in the same relationship to our present selves as our own future interests.[3] So, it might appear that Nagel's internalism would also predict the correlation. However, while our future interests may give us reasons to act now, they do not give us the ability to ensure that we act in accordance with those interests. What matters is not whether we have reasons to act in our long-term interests or whether we can recognize those reasons but whether we have the ability to act on the reasons we recognize. Similarly, while the interests of others may give us reason to act, they do not automatically enable us to do so.

No other theory explicitly predicts the three states of affairs under discussion. There are certainly no other by-product theories that do and, as I argued in chapter 1, the truth about human morality probably has to be a by-product theory. It does not follow that evolutionary intuitionism is the final word in ethics. For one thing, as is normally the case with empirical theories, it cannot be conclusively confirmed. For another, there are empirical tests yet to be carried out. For instance, we would have to try to determine empirically whether moral judges from different cultures would agree in their moral judgments when the factors that distort intuitions were absent. If they disagreed, we would have to reject the theory. Finally, I have not proved that the theory explains everything moral. The fact that the theory has no unacceptably counter-intuitive implications shows that it is "sound," but it does not show that it is "complete." If it is not "complete," it might need to be supplemented by other foundational attitudes.

The fact that some theories do not explain the empirical observations should enable us to shorten our list of plausible alternatives. Hence, even though evolutionary intuitionism may not be the final word in ethics, it does contribute to our understanding of human morality. We have made progress. Indeed, the fact that no other theory makes the same predictions provides some evidence that evolutionary intuitionism is the only one that can. It is not conclusive evidence, because I have not gone to the trouble to show that no other theory could possibly do so. However, if only evolutionary intuitionism, as a matter of fact, does explain the observations, then provisionally we have reason to prefer evolutionary intuitionism to its competitors. A good theory can of course be replaced by a better one. But the replacement would have to predict everything that evolutionary intuitionism predicts, together with some additional facts.

THEORETICAL VIRTUES OF EVOLUTIONARY INTUITIONISM

Evolutionary intuitionism is a theory in the sense in which the theory of evolution is a theory. A good scientific theory should be testable: it should predict phenomena that it was not designed to explain. Evolutionary intuitionism is testable in this sense – it was not, for instance, designed to explain reflexive rationalization. It has passed the tests so far. It has other virtues of good scientific theories as well.

First, evolutionary intuitionism is conservative: it is consistent with standard scientific views. It is orthodox to hold that heritable variation and natural selection explain biological characteristics. Evolutionary biology is itself consistent with the full range of the sciences. However, the theory does not sacrifice ethical plausibility for the sake of scientific respectability. Ethical intuitionism is a conservative meta-ethical position. Evolutionary intuitionism provides a new basis for a form of it. The moral facts postulated may not be quite what most intuitionists expected but that is no objection. The new theory does not require us to alter our conception of ethical intuitionism substantially.

Second, evolutionary intuitionism has the widest possible scope for a theory designed to explain human morality. It encompasses meta-ethics, normative ethics, and moral motivation. No other theory clearly does so.

Third, evolutionary intuitionism is a simple theory. It postulates the existence of only one new kind of entity, foundational attitudes. Moreover, they are not utterly novel but closely resemble beliefs. Foundational attitudes are no stranger than false beliefs that originate for psychological reasons that have nothing to do with the truth. The concept of value* is reducible to a set of more familiar concepts. Moral facts are constructed out of acts, foundational attitudes, consistency, and concepts. The structures created out of the elements are new but the elements themselves are mostly familiar.

The posited arrangement of adaptations is also simple. It includes the foundational attitude that one is of value*, the disposition to acknowledge some others as being of value*, the extended foundational attitude that others are of value*, the commitment to regard all other possessors as being of value*, and the ways in which foundational attitudes are contingent upon our being able to desire certain ends when we act. The only other factors are *akrasia*, reflexive rationalization, our tendency to believe truly about our acts, and our inclination to maintain consistency between our foundational attitude and our beliefs.

Evolutionary intuitionism is highly coherent because of its scope and its simplicity. Theorists can gerrymander their theories to cover everything they should cover. However, if they do so to avoid falsification or to increase the scope of a theory, the theory is unlikely to be simple. The coherence that results from the combination of scope and simplicity is evidence for the truth of evolutionary intuitionism because the best explanation for it is that the theory is true. When that evidence is combined with the argument that human morality must be an evolutionary by-product, the case for evolutionary intuitionism is strong.

It might be argued that evolutionary intuitionism is not fruitful because it has not led to the observation of any hitherto unknown phenomena. We knew that every human society had a moral code. We knew that people sometimes rationalized when they had no apparent reason for doing so. We knew that psychopaths were both amoral and unconcerned about the future. We knew that different societies tended to have different moral codes. While this is all true, it is not important. As a theory goes from success to success, we should expect it to become less fruitful because the world is finite and there is not an endless supply of new kinds of phenomena to be discovered or explained. In fact, we should expect even the best theories to cease to be fruitful. While fruitfulness provides a reason to keep working on a problematic theory or to prefer one theory to another, increasing lack of fruitfulness is no reason to reject a theory that has already achieved success. I am not claiming that evolutionary intuitionism has been fruitful but only pointing out that lack of fruitfulness does not necessarily mean that a theory is defective.

As for the fact that evolutionary intuitionism has not led to new observations, the moral world is a very small world and of great concern to human beings. It should not be surprising that everything significant has been observed before theory construction commences. Moreover, even if it is not particularly fruitful, it may be no worse off than any other theory of human morality. Finally, the temporal element is irrelevant when there is a theory that enables us to expect and explain phenomena that we actually observe – retrodictions are as good as predictions and the intrinsic quality of theories cannot be undermined by historical accidents of discovery. Overall, in a reasonable assessment, the theory's apparent lack of fruitfulness would not outweigh its virtues.

Less defensively, I can say that evolutionary intuitionism was fruitful for me. I developed the evolutionary explanation for the development of foundational attitudes before I knew anything about psychopaths. When I realized that amoral human beings should be bad at long-term planning if my explanation was correct, I investigated and discovered that they were. The theory thus led me to observe a fact that I had not known about, one that I did not design the theory to explain. My experience was similar with respect to reflexive rationalization. Although I knew that people rationalized to escape punishment, I did not know that they did so for other reasons.

A PLAUSIBLE REALISM

As a form of realism, evolutionary intuitionism takes an intermediate position. On the one hand, moral facts are not so removed from human beings that our awareness of them and their influence on us are mysterious. They are facts but facts with which we have an intimate relationship. On the other hand, they are not so close to us that morality becomes subjective. The facts do not vary with our whims, preferences, desires, or opinions. Our obligations are categorical imperatives rather than hypothetical imperatives. The fact that the theory postulates moral facts that are both objective and accessible is in its favour. I believe that the moral facts are precisely where we should have expected to discover them.

The theory posits real normativity. "Being of value*" is a normative concept that infuses the moral facts themselves with normativity. From the point of view of someone who holds a desire-dependent extended foundational attitude, it is true that he ought to rescue his neighbour if his neighbour is in danger. The reason, although it is not consciously expressed, is that his neighbour is of value*. That is how he must see it, because he is committed to regard his neighbour as valuable*. But it is not just a matter of seeing his neighbour as valuable*. Because of his foundational attitude and the commitments that they entail, it is true that he ought to save his neighbour. It is true because of his nature, his neighbour's nature, and their relationship. Not even the realization that foundational attitudes are false can alter the situation. Since they are not beliefs and are therefore not defective even if false, awareness of their falsity does not result in their rejection.

The theory shows how moral facts could originate in a purely physical world governed by natural laws as we know them. It explains how moral normativity could enter into a physical world and come to have a grip on biological organisms. Indeed, there seems to be no other way for genuine moral normativity, at least of the sort the intuitionist believes in, to enter a world with the physical and biological features that our world possesses. But even if it is not the only way, the possibility of moral normativity arising in a purely physical world among purely physical organisms reduces the temptation to indulge in metaphysical speculation. Ethical realists can see the world as a unified whole. Evolutionary intuitionism makes ethics part of the natural world without destroying its distinctiveness by reducing moral properties completely to non-moral properties. Evolutionary intuitionism naturalizes morality; it does not denature it.

FINAL REMARKS

Reacting to adaptationist evolutionary ethics, some commentators have concluded that Darwinism makes the world a bleak and depressing place. To repeat a quotation from the first chapter, "if one consistently adhered to the Darwinist canon, the logical social ethic (beyond being merely egocentric) would be to join with genetically kindred persons to get the better, reproductively, of all others, ultimately to replace them by whatever means available."[4] The writer assumes that evolutionary competition results in ethnic, tribal, and inter-familial conflict and assumes that Darwinism can only approve of it. Certainly, natural selection brings about such conflict. There is a case to be made that we can expect no more if ethics is the product of group selection, kin selection, or reciprocal altruism. If adaptationist evolutionary ethics were the only evolutionary possibility, the bleak and depressing view would be plausible.

Since there are also by-product theories like evolutionary intuitionism, however, the quotation is at best an overstatement and at worst plain false. There is more than one kind of "kinship." Genetically, every human moral agent is "kin" to every other human moral agent, because every human moral agent shares the genetic basis of his moral agency with every other human moral agent. Hence, it is not entirely metaphorical to speak of other human beings as one's brothers and sisters. But we need not stop there. Organisms with foundational attitudes could benefit from co-operation with other organisms with foundational attitudes whether they share a common ancestor or not. Ultimately, morality becomes free of its biological origin within a species with a particular evolutionary history. It is as independent of our specifically biological interests as any objective ethics could be.

We do not have to fear that we will evolve to be amoral. Throughout our time on this planet, moral agents have combined to get the better of all others. Morality and some selective processes do clash. It is a conflict between one aspect of our biological nature and another in which morality has won again and again. The new Adam battles the old Adam and triumphs repeatedly – although it is true that the old Adam is never totally and finally vanquished. Morality wins for good evolutionary reasons. It wins because it is connected to an adaptation that enables moral agents to gain despite the fact that morality itself imposes a cost.

Human morality is a by-product of evolution by heritable variation and natural selection. It is fully part of the natural world but is none the worse for that – on the contrary. In the last sentence of *On the Origin of Species*, Darwin declares that "there is grandeur in this view of life ... [on which] endless forms most beautiful and most wonderful have been, and are being evolved."[5] The beautiful and wonderful forms include true moral agents who respond to real moral facts and who form a natural moral community. Their existence contributes to the grandeur of Darwin's evolutionary view of life.

Notes

CHAPTER ONE

1 For the locus classicus of broader attacks see Gould and Lewontin, "The Spandrels of San Marco," and Gould, *The Structure of Evolutionary Theory.*
2 Mayr, "How to Carry Out the Adaptationist Program?" 282.
3 Darwin, *The Descent of Man.*
4 Ruse, *Taking Darwin Seriously.*
5 Sober, *Philosophy of Biology*, 90 (italics in original).
6 Sterelny and Griffiths, *Sex and Death*, 153.
7 With the publication by Williams of his *Adaptation and Natural Selection.*
8 See Thompson, "Evolutionary Ethics: Its Origin and Contemporary Face."
9 Sober and Wilson, *Unto Others.*
10 Gilbert, *The Righteous*, 443.
11 See Tec, "Reflections on Rescuers."
12 Some rescuers of Jews were motivated by commercial considerations (see Tec, "Reflections on Rescuers"). Not all Ukrainian rescuers were motivated in that way, however. (see Hunczak, "Ukrainian-Jewish Relations during the Soviet and Nazi Occupations"). As of 1 January 2005, Yad Vashem counted 2,079 persons from Ukraine among the Righteous among the Nations, people who tried to save Jews without a view to gain and for whose efforts evidence exists (see www1.yadvashem.org/righteous/indexrighteous.html).
13 Krawchenko, "Soviet Ukraine under Nazi Occupation, 1941–44," 29.
14 Weiss, "The Holocaust and Ukrainian Victims," 113.
15 Berkhoff, *Harvest of Despair*, 85.

16 See Hunczak, "The Ukrainian Losses during World War II."
17 Berkhoff, *Harvest of Despair*, 85. Berkhoff seems to be mistaken. Two people were arrested, but one was released soon after. The other was in a forced labour camp for eight months (see Tec, *When Light Pierced the Darkness*). Nonetheless, there was a dramatic difference in the severity of the punishment.
18 See Monroe, Barton, and Klingemann, "Altruism and the Theory of Rational Action: Rescuers of Jews in Nazi Europe."
19 See Tec, *When Light Pierced the Darkness*.
20 Ruse, "Is Rape Wrong on Andromeda?" 69.
21 Ruse, *Taking Darwin Seriously*, 244.
22 Ibid., 240.
23 Ibid., 242.
24 Ibid., 271.
25 For example, see Goodenough and Deacon, "From Biology to Consciousness to Morality."
26 Gould, *The Structure of Evolutionary Theory*, 1247 (italics in original). With respect to this particular issue, Gould declares that he "accept[s]the standard view" that the quoted statement expresses.
27 Sober and Wilson, *Unto Others*, 9 (italics in original).
28 Ibid., 326.
29 Ibid., 174.
30 Trivers, "The Evolution of Reciprocal Altruism," 49.
31 Ibid., 37.
32 Alexander, "A Biological Interpretation of Moral Systems," 188.
33 Alexander, *The Biology of Moral Systems*, 94.
34 See Tec, "Reflections on Rescuers."
35 Alexander, *The Biology of Moral Systems*, 94.
36 See Frank, *Passions within Reason*.
37 Richards, "Darwin's Romantic Biology," 144.
38 Wesson, *Beyond Natural Selection*, 307.
39 Manipulation of the kind discussed by Lee Cronk ("Evolutionary Theories of Morality and the Manipulative Use of Signals") is a misfiring. The fact that one organism induces the misfiring in another does not make it a different kind of thing. Neither does selection for the ability to induce misfirings.
40 See Ruse and Wilson, "Moral Philosophy as Applied Science."
41 See Boyd and Richerson, *Culture and the Evolutionary Process*.
42 See Sober, *Philosophy of Biology*.
43 See Cavalli-Sforza and Feldman, *Cultural Transmission and Evolution*.

44 See Boyd and Richerson, "Punishment Allows the Evolution of Cooperation (or Anything Else)."

45 Sober and Wilson, *Unto Others*, 155 (italics in original).

46 Ibid., 171.

47 Tec, "Reflections on Rescuers," 655.

48 Ibid., 655–6.

49 Gilbert, *The Righteous*, 438.

50 Richerson and Boyd, *Not by Genes Alone*, 125.

51 See www1.yadvashem.org/righteous/indexrighteous.html.

52 Ayala, "The Biological Roots of Morality," 237.

53 Ibid.

54 See Sesardic, "Recent Work on Human Altruism and Evolution."

55 The example of bitter substances is taken from Richerson and Boyd, *Not by Genes Alone*.

56 The distinction between selection *for* and selection *of* a feature was made by Sober in *The Nature of Selection*.

CHAPTER TWO

1 See Hudson, *Ethical Intuitionism*, for an account of the characteristic features of ethical intuitionism.

2 Williams, "Deciding to Believe," 136.

3 See Adler, "The Ethics of Belief: Off the Wrong Track"; Humberstone, "Direction of Fit"; Jones, "Explaining Our Beliefs"; Leon, "Responsible Believers"; and J. David Velleman, "On the Aim of Belief."

4 See Clark, *Paradoxes from A to Z*.

5 I shall not be discussing the question of whether death is bad, like Nagel in his "Death" or McMahan in his "Death and the Value of Life."

6 For my purposes, it is not necessary to explain the conditions that determine whether we act consistently with a proposition and its negation or whether we act consistently with a proposition and inconsistently with its negation.

7 It is a disposition to maintain consistency, not a disposition to maintain what we believe to be consistency. It is unclear what evidence would count for or against the latter. We could believe any set of beliefs to be consistent. In contrast, there could be evidence for or against a disposition to maintain objective consistency. Sufficient inconsistency would disprove its existence. What I imagine the disposition to be is some sort of "mechanism" that sorts our beliefs appropriately and that generally prevents inconsistency. I do not imagine that it is perfect. Rather,

I suppose that most of the time the automatic sorting process works and we are unaware of its operation. When it fails, we sometimes compensate "manually" by consciously exploring the implications of beliefs. The way in which we make the occasional correction is not the way in which consistency is ordinarily maintained, however.

8 See Gewirth, *Reason and Morality.*

CHAPTER THREE

1 Darwin, *The Descent of Man*, 102.

2 See Stingl, "All the Monkeys Aren't in the Zoo."

3 Walker, in his *Animal Thought*, points out that no experimental evidence shows that animals have much interest in the future. Researchers like Griffin (*Animal Minds*) provide plenty of evidence that animals are capable of what appears to be intelligent, rational thought, but they do not give us any examples that would indicate that non-humans can plan for the future, let alone carry out the plans.

4 See Sterelny and Griffiths, *Sex and Death.*

5 By assuming the existence of social rules and norms that are not moral rules I am not multiplying kinds of entities unnecessarily. Systems of laws are systems of social rules and norms, but the law is distinct from morality. Furthermore, rules and norms that exist to maintain class distinctions are not moral rules; neither are the rules and norms of criminal organizations.

6 Dawkins, *The Selfish Gene*, 89.

7 Brown, *Human Universals*, 139.

8 See Turnbull, *The Mountain People.*

9 See Heine, "The Mountain People: Some Notes on the Ik of North-Eastern Uganda."

10 Redfield, *The Primitive World and Its Transformation*, 15.

11 See Sykes and Matza, "Techniques of Neutralization: A Theory of Delinquency."

12 See Festinger, *A Theory of Cognitive Dissonance.*

13 See Aronson, *The Social Animal.*

14 See Stephenson, *The Psychology of Criminal Justice.*

15 See Aronson, *The Social Animal.*

16 See Hafner and Boker, *Crimes of Violence by Mentally Abnormal Offenders.*

17 Hare, *Without Conscience*, 40–1.

18 Cleckley, *The Mask of Sanity*, 364.
19 Ibid., 345.
20 Stout, *The Sociopath Next Door*, 189–90. I have substituted "psychopath" for the synonymous "sociopath" in the quotation. Stout uses the terms interchangeably.
21 See Harpur, Hart, and Hare, "The Personality of the Psychopath."
22 See Swanson, Bland, and Newman, "Antisocial Personality Disorders."
23 See Robins, Tipp, and Przybeck, "Antisocial Personality."
24 Hart and Hare, "Psychopathy: Assessment and Association with Criminal Conduct," 24.
25 Hare, *Without Conscience*, 59.
26 See Schulsinger, "Psychopathy: Heredity and Environment"; Harris, *The Nurture Assumption*; and Viding, Blair, Moffit, and Plomin, "Evidence for Substantial Genetic Risk for Psychopathy in Seven-Year-Olds."
27 See Rowe, "Inherited Dispositions toward Learning Delinquent and Criminal Behavior."
28 Ellis, "The Evolution of Violent Criminal Behavior," 73.

CHAPTER FOUR

1 When I speak of prima facie obligations, I mean merely the obligations a person has provided that there is a desire-dependent way of fulfilling them but that he may not have if there is no such way, given the particular circumstances he is in. I do not mean prima facie obligations of the sort proposed by Ross in *The Right and the Good*.
2 If our use of resources means that some who actually come into existence in the future would suffer, then either we have an obligation to restrain ourselves in using them, provided that we do not thereby transfer the suffering to ourselves, or we have an obligation to limit the number of those who actually come into existence in the future.
3 Sometimes, we are committed to increase the quantity of something that is instrumentally valuable because increasing it is necessary to preserve the valuable*. For instance, we may be committed to increase the amount of a particular vaccine available because we can thereby minimize the number of deaths that the vaccine is intended to prevent. Such cases do not show that principles of maximizing or satisficing are true with respect to the valuable*.
4 Acting without someone's consent can sometimes be justified, but the kind of case under discussion is not one in which it is. We are sometimes

justified in doing things without someone's consent when it is to his benefit and he is in our care. For example, we can sometimes administer foul-tasting medicine to children despite their protests. Sometimes, we are justified when, otherwise, someone would do something impermissible. We do not require the consent of an embezzler before we confiscate his ill-gotten gains. Sometimes, we can act without someone's consent when he deserves what happens to him, such as when he is punished for a crime. However, there is no such justification for overriding someone's not consenting to die for others. Because the sacrifice is not for the benefit of the sacrificed, it is permissible for the sacrificial victim to prevent himself from being sacrificed, even if he must kill those intent on sacrificing him in order to save his own life. Finally, he does not deserve to die. Even if he did deserve to die for some crime or other, there would be no justification. That someone has stolen makes him liable to make restitution or to suffer punishment; it does not make him fair game for other thieves. In short, the sorts of moral reasons that justify overriding a lack of consent are not present.

5 Disrupting the arrangement is not a case of killing an innocent threat, the prospective beneficiary, in order to preserve another, even though death ensues. One can often both disrupt the arrangement and take steps intended to preserve the erstwhile prospective beneficiary even if the steps are not successful.

6 Killing someone who was attempting suicide would be content-consistent because, by making the attempt, the would-be suicide victim would eliminate his foundational attitude. Thus, if someone was trying to kill himself using one of Dr Kevorkian's contraptions and if the machine failed to do the job, someone could complete what the would-be suicide victim was trying to do. Until he was actually trying to end his own life, however, everyone would have an obligation to preserve him, to do whatever was possible to maintain his desire to avoid injury.

7 See Stephenson, *The Psychology of Criminal Justice.*

8 This is the case no matter who the victim is. No one has an obligation to endure an abusive relationship with their offspring or with their parents. An abusive relative cannot claim a right to be supported by his victim anymore than an abusive stranger can. Of course, our reactions must be proportionate in this kind of case as well. Although we probably have an obligation to subsidize abusive parents who are elderly and indigent, we probably do not have an obligation to permit them to live with us. We certainly do not have a duty to allow them opportunities to abuse us.

CHAPTER FIVE

1 Darwall, "Internalism and Agency," 155 (italics in original).
2 If he makes a moral judgment with someone else as the subject and if the other fails to act in accordance with the judgment, he may make another moral judgment with himself as the subject, a judgment about what he ought to do because the other has not done what he ought to do. The latter judgment is not to be confused with the judgment he makes with the other as the subject.
3 Their conclusions about actual cases would usually have the same truth-value, except if they were in relevantly similar circumstances, in which case their moral judgments about what each should do would not have the same truth-value. The one without a foundational attitude might conclude that he himself ought to do something, but it would not be the case that he ought to do it because of his lack of a foundational attitude. The one with a foundational attitude in the same situation would also conclude that he himself ought to do something, and his conclusion would be true. The relevant difference is not in the external circumstances but in the possession of or lack of a foundational attitude.
4 Brink, *Moral Realism and the Foundations of Ethics*, 46 (italics in original).
5 Ibid.
6 For a discussion of the present state of knowledge about human memory, see Schachter, *The Seven Sins of Memory.*
7 Ibid.
8 See Gilovich, *How We Know What Isn't So.*

CHAPTER SIX

1 Mackie, *Ethics: Inventing Right and Wrong*, 38.
2 See Hume, *A Treatise of Human Nature.*
3 Sober, "Prospects for an Evolutionary Ethics," 103 (italics in original).
4 Ibid., 109 (italics in original).
5 See Darwin, *The Descent of Man.*
6 Since foundational attitudes cannot be introspected, people who sincerely state that they are worthless do not thereby provide conclusive evidence that they lack foundational attitudes.
7 See Quirk, Greenbaum, Leech, and Svartvik, *A Comprehensive Grammar of the English Language*. This is not the only case in which it is

necessary to posit beliefs that the believer cannot introspect in order to explain his linguistic behaviour. For instance, whether one uses a definite or an indefinite noun phrase depends on what one believes about the knowledge of the people to whom one is speaking. If one thinks that one's listeners know what one is referring to, one uses the definite. If one is introducing something new, one uses the indefinite.

8 See Williams, *Ethics and the Limits of Philosophy*.

9 Mackie, *Ethics: Inventing Right and Wrong*, 38.

10 See Dretske, "Conclusive Reasons."

11 Smith, *The Moral Problem*, 2 (italics in original).

12 See Ruse and Wilson, "Moral Philosophy as Applied Science"; Geiger, "Why There Are No Objective Values"; Geiger, "Evolutionary Anthropology and the Non-Cognitive Foundation of Moral Validity"; and Joyce, "Darwinian Ethics and Error."

13 See Collier and Stingl, "Evolutionary Naturalism and the Objectivity of Morality"; Campbell, "Can Biology Make Ethics Objective?" and Harms, "Adaptation and Moral Realism."

14 Campbell, "Can Biology Make Ethics Objective?" 25.

15 Mackie, *Ethics: Inventing Right and Wrong*, 49.

16 Ibid., 43.

17 Ibid.

18 Ruse and Wilson, "Moral Philosophy as Applied Science," 179.

19 Ibid., 186.

CHAPTER SEVEN

1 Sesardic, "Recent Work on Human Altruism and Evolution," 144.

2 Harman, *The Nature of Morality*, 10.

3 See Nagel, *The Possibility of Altruism*.

4 Wesson, *Beyond Natural Selection*, 307.

5 Darwin, *On the Origin of Species*, 347.

Bibliography

Adler, Jonathan E. "The Ethics of Belief: Off the Wrong Track." *Midwest Studies in Philosophy* 23 (1999): 267–85.

Alexander, Richard D. "Biological Considerations in the Analysis of Morality." In Matthew H. Nitecki and Doris V. Nitecki, eds., *Evolutionary Ethics*. Albany, NY: State University of New York Press 1993, 163–96.

– "A Biological Interpretation of Moral Systems." In Paul Thompson, ed., *Issues in Evolutionary Ethics*. Albany, NY: State University of New York Press 1995, 179-202. Rpt. from *Zygon* 20 (1985): 3–20.

– *The Biology of Moral Systems*. New York: Aldine de Gruyter 1987.

Aronson, Elliot. *The Social Animal*. 5th ed. New York: W.H. Freeman 1988.

Arrington, Robert. *Rationalism, Realism, and Relativism: Perspectives in Contemporary Moral Epistemology*. Ithaca, NY: Cornell University Press 1989.

Ayala, Francisco J. "The Biological Roots of Morality." *Biology and Philosophy* 2 (1987): 235–52.

– "The Difference of Being Human." In Holmes Rolston III, ed., *Biology, Ethics and the Origin of Life*. Boston: Jones and Bartlett 1995, 117–35.

Barrett, Jonathan. "Really Taking Darwin and the Naturalistic Fallacy Seriously." *Biology and Philosophy* 6 (1991): 433–7.

Bayles, Michael D. "Intuitions in Ethics." *Dialogue* 23 (1984): 439–55.

Bekoff, Marc. "Wild Justice and Fair play: Cooperation, Forgiveness, and Morality in Animals." *Biology and Philosophy* 19 (2004): 489–520.

Bennett, Jonathan. "Why Is Belief Involuntary?" *Analysis* 50 (1990): 87–107.

Berkhoff, Karel C. *Harvest of Despair: Life and Death in Ukraine under Nazi Rule*. Cambridge, MA, and London: The Belknap Press of Harvard University Press 2004.

Bilgrami, Akeel. *Belief and Meaning: The Unity and Locality of Mental Content*. Oxford: Blackwell 1992.

Bogdan, Radu J. *Belief: Form, Content and Function*. Oxford: Clarendon Press 1986.

– "Common Sense Naturalized: The Practical Stance." In Radu J. Bogdan, ed., *Mind and Common Sense: Philosophical Essays on Commonsense Psychology*. Cambridge: Cambridge University Press 1991, 161–206.

– "The Importance of Belief." In Radu J. Bogdan, ed., *Mind and Common Sense: Philosophical Essays on Commonsense Psychology*. Cambridge: Cambridge University Press 1991, 1–16.

– "The Manufacture of Belief." In Radu J. Bogdan, ed., *Mind and Common Sense: Philosophical Essays on Commonsense Psychology*. Cambridge: Cambridge University Press 1991, 149–84.

Bohannan, Paul. *Justice and Judgement among the Tiv*. London: Oxford University Press 1968.

Boyd, Robert, and Peter Richerson. *Culture and the Evolutionary Process*. Chicago: University of Chicago Press 1985.

– "Punishment Allows the Evolution of Cooperation (or Anything Else)." In Robert Boyd and Peter Richerson, *The Origin and Evolution of Cultures*. Oxford: Oxford University Press 2005, 166–88. Rpt. from *Ethology and Sociobiology* 13 (1992): 171–95.

Bradie, Michael. *The Secret Chain: Evolution and Ethics*. Albany, NY: State University of New York Press 1994.

Braithwaite, R.B. "The Nature of Believing." *Proceedings of the Aristotelian Society* 33 (1932–33): 129–46.

Brink, David O. *Moral Realism and the Foundations of Ethics*. Cambridge: Cambridge University Press 1989.

Brown, Donald E. *Human Universals*. Philadelphia: Temple University Press 1991.

Bull, Stephen W. "Gibbard's Evolutionary Theory of Rationality and Its Evolutionary Implications." *Biology and Philosophy* 10 (1995): 129–80.

Cain, A.J. "The True Meaning of Darwinian Evolution." In Alan Grafen, ed., *Evolution and Its Influence*. Oxford: Clarendon Press 1989, 1–18.

Campbell, Richmond. "Can Biology Make Ethics Objective?" *Biology and Philosophy* 11 (1996): 21–31.

Cavalli-Sforza, L., and M. Feldman. *Cultural Transmission and Evolution: A Quantitative Approach*. Princeton: Princeton University Press 1981.

Cela-Conde, Camilo J. "The Challenge of Evolutionary Ethics." *Biology and Philosophy* 1 (1986): 293–7.

Chagnon, Napoleon A. *Yanomamo: The Fierce People*. 3d ed. New York: Holt, Rinehart and Winston 1983.

Chapanis, N.J., and A.C. Chapanis. "Cognitive Dissonance: Five Years Later." *Psychological Bulletin* 61 (1964): 1–22.

Churchland, Paul M. "Folk Psychology and the Explanation of Human Behavior." In Radu J. Bogdan, ed., *Mind and Common Sense: Philosophical Essays on Commonsense Psychology*. Cambridge: Cambridge University Press 1991: 37–52.

Clark, Michael. *Paradoxes from A to Z*. London and New York: Routledge 2002.

Clark, Stephen R.L. "Have Biologists Wrapped Up Philosophy?" *Inquiry* 43 (2000): 143–66.

Cleckley, Hervey. *The Mask of Sanity*. 5th ed. Saint Louis: C.V. Mosby 1976.

Cling, Andrew D. "The Empirical Virtues of Beliefs." *Philosophical Psychology* 4 (1991): 303–23.

Cohen, L. Jonathan. "Belief and Acceptance." *Mind* 98 (1989): 367–89.

Collier, John, and Michael Stingl. "Evolutionary Naturalism and the Objectivity of Morality." *Biology and Philosophy* 8 (1993): 47–60.

Crimmins, Mark. *Talk about Belief*. Cambridge, MA: MIT Press 1992.

Cronk, Lee. "Evolutionary Theories of Morality and the Manipulative Use of Signals." *Zygon* 29 (1994): 81–101.

Cummins, Robert. "Methodological Reflections on Belief." In Radu J. Bogdan, ed., *Mind and Common Sense: Philosophical Essays on Commonsense Psychology*. Cambridge: Cambridge University Press 1991, 53–70.

Daniels, Norman. "Moral Theory and the Plasticity of Persons." *The Monist* 62 (1979): 265–87.

Darwall, Stephen L. "Internalism and Agency." *Philosophical Perspectives* 6 (1992): 155–74.

Darwin, Charles. *The Descent of Man, and Selection in Relation to Sex, Part One*. Ed. Paul H. Barrett and R.B. Freeman. New York: New York University Press 1989.

– "Moral Sense." In Paul Thompson, ed., *Issues in Evolutionary Ethics*. Albany, NY: State University of New York Press 1995, 41–76. From *The Descent of Man and Selection in Relation to Race*. 2d ed. London: John Murray 1874, 148–94.

– *On the Origin of Species*. Ed. Paul H. Barrett and R.B. Freeman. New York: New York University Press 1988.

Dawkins, Richard. *The Blind Watchmaker*. Harmondsworth, England: Penguin 1988.

– *The Selfish Gene*. New edition. Oxford: Oxford University Press 1989.

Dennett, Daniel C. "Beyond Belief." In Andrew Woodfield, ed., *Thought and Object: Essays on Intentionality*. Oxford: Clarendon Press 1982, 1–95.

– *Darwin's Dangerous Idea: Evolution and the Meanings of Life*. New York: Simon and Schuster 1995.

de Waal, Franz. *Good Natured: The Origins of Right and Wrong in Humans and Others Animals*. Cambridge, MA: Harvard University Press 1996.

Dodder, Richard, and Stella P. Hughes. "Collegiate Drinking Behavior: A Test of Neutralization Theory." *Journal of Alcohol and Drug Education* 33 (1987): 73–85.

Dretske, Fred. "Conclusive Reasons." *Australasian Journal of Philosophy* 49 (1971): 1–22.

– *Explaining Behavior: Reasons in a World of Causes*. Cambridge, MA: MIT Press 1988.

Dunn, Judy. "The Beginnings of Moral Understanding: Development in the Second Year." In Jerome Kagan and Sharon Lamb, eds., *The Emergence of Morality in Young Children*. Chicago: University of Chicago Press 1987, 91–112.

Elliott, Carl, and Grant Gillett. "Moral Insanity and Practical Reason." *Philosophical Psychology* 5 (1992): 53–67.

Ellis, Lee. "The Evolution of Violent Criminal Behavior and Its Non-Legal Equivalent." In Lee Ellis and Harry Hoffman, eds., *Crime in Biological, Social, and Moral Contexts*. New York: Praeger 1990, 61–80.

Endler, John A. *Natural Selection in the Wild*. Princeton: Princeton University Press 1986.

Eysenck, H.J. *Crime and Personality*. 3d ed. London: Routledge and Kegan Paul 1977.

Feldman, Shel. *Cognitive Consistency: Motivational Antecedents and Behavioral Consequents*. New York: Academic Press 1966.

Festinger, Leon. *A Theory of Cognitive Dissonance*. Stanford, CA: Stanford University Press 1957.

Flanagan, Owen J. "Is Morality Epiphenomenal? The Failure of the Sociobiological Reduction of Ethics." *The Philosophical Forum* 13 (1981–82): 207–25.

Fogelman, Eva. "The Rescuer Self." In Michael Berenbaum and Abraham J. Peck, eds., *The Holocaust and History: The Known, the Unknown, the Disputed, and the Reexamined*. Bloomington, IN: Indiana University Press 1998, 663–77.

Foot, Phillippa. "Morality, Action, and Outcome." In Ted Honderich, ed. *Morality and Objectivity.* London: Routledge and Kegan Paul 1985, 23–38.

Frank, Robert H. *Passions within Reason: The Strategic Role of the Emotions.* New York and London: W.W. Norton 1988.

Furnish, Victor. "Love of Neighbor in the New Testament." *Journal of Religious Ethics* 10 (1982): 327–34.

Garfield, Jay L. *Belief in Psychology: A Study in the Ontology of Mind.* Cambridge, MA: MIT Press 1988.

Gauthier, David. *Morals by Agreement.* Oxford: Clarendon Press 1986.

Geiger, Gebhard. "Evolutionary Anthropology and the Non-Cognitive Foundation of Moral Validity." *Biology and Philosophy* 8 (1993): 133–51.

– "Why There Are No Objective Values: A Critique of Ethical Intuitionism from a Biological Point of View." *Biology and Philosophy* 7 (1992): 315–30.

Gewirth, Alan. "How Ethical Is Evolutionary Ethics?" In Matthew H. Nitecki and Doris V. Nitecki, eds., *Evolutionary Ethics.* Albany: State University of New York Press 1993, 241–56.

– "The Problem of Specificity in Evolutionary Ethics." *Biology and Philosophy* 1 (1986): 297–305.

– *Reason and Morality.* Chicago: University of Chicago Press 1978.

Gibbard, Allan. *Wise Choices, Apt Feelings.* Cambridge, MA: Harvard University Press 1990.

Gilbert, Martin. *The Righteous: The Unsung Heroes of the Holocaust.* New York: Henry Holt 2003.

Gilovich, Thomas. *How We Know What Isn't So: The Fallibility of Human Reason in Everyday Life.* New York: The Free Press 1991.

Glover, Jonathan. *Humanity: A Moral History of the Twentieth Century.* London: Jonathan Cape 1999.

Gluckmann, Max, ed. *Ideas and Procedures in African Customary Law.* London: Oxford University Press 1969.

Goodenough, Ursula, and Terrence W. Deacon. "From Biology to Consciousness to Morality." *Zygon* 38 (2003): 801–19.

Gould, Stephen Jay. "Sociobiology and the Theory of Natural Selection." In Michael Ruse, ed., *Philosophy of Biology.* New York: Macmillan 1989, 253–63.

– *The Structure of Evolutionary Theory.* Cambridge, MA and London: The Belknap Press of Harvard University Press 2002.

Gould, Stephen Jay, and Richard Lewontin. "The Spandrels of San Marco." In David R. Keller and Frank B. Golley, eds., *The Philosophy of Ecology: From Science to Synthesis.* Athens, GA, and London: The

University of Georgia Press 2000, 263–76. Rpt. from *Proceedings of the Royal Society of London: Biological Sciences* 205 (1979): 581–98.

Gould, Stephen Jay, and Elisabeth S. Vrba. "Exaptation: A Missing Term in the Philosophy of Science." *Paleobiology* 8 (1982): 4–15.

Grice, Paul. *The Conception of Value*. Oxford: Clarendon Press 1991.

Griffin, Donald R. *Animal Minds*. Chicago: University of Chicago Press 1992.

Griffin, James. "The Ambitions of Consequentialism." *Social Philosophy and Policy* 9 (1992): 118–32.

Griffiths, A. Phillips. "On Belief." *Proceedings of the Aristotelian Society* 63 (1962–63): 167–86.

Hafner, H., and W. Boker. *Crimes of Violence by Mentally Abnormal Offenders: A Psychiatric and Epidemiological Study in the Federal German Republic*. Cambridge: Cambridge University Press 1982.

Hare, Robert D. "Comparison of Procedure for the Assessment of Psychopathy." *Journal of Consulting and Clinical Psychology* 53 (1985): 7–16.

– "A Research Scale for the Assessment of Psychopathy in Criminal Populations." *Personal and Individual Differences* 1 (1980): 111–19.

– *Without Conscience: The Disturbing World of the Psychopaths among Us*. New York: Pocket Books 1993.

Hare, Robert D., and John F. Connolly. "Perceptual Asymmetries and Information Processing in Psychopaths." In Sarnoff A. Mednick, Terrie E. Moffit, and Susan A. Stack, eds., *The Causes of Crime: New Biological Approaches*. Cambridge: Cambridge University Press 1987, 218–38.

Hare, Robert D., Timothy J. Harpur, A.R. Hakstian, Adelle E. Forth, Stephen D. Hart, and Joseph P. Newman. "The Revised Psychopathy Checklist: Reliability and Factor Structure." *Psychological Assessment: A Journal of Consulting and Clinical Psychology* 2 (1990): 338–41.

Hare, Robert D., Sherrie E. Williamson, and Timothy J. Harpur. "Psychopathy and Language." In Terrie E. Moffit and Sarnoff A. Mednick, eds., *Biological Contributions to Crime Causation*. Dordrecht: Martinus Nijhoff Publishers 1988, 68–92.

Harman, Gilbert. "Is There a Single True Morality?" In Michael Krausz, ed., *Relativism: Interpretation and Confrontation*. Notre Dame, IN: University of Notre Dame Press 1989, 363–89.

– *The Nature of Morality*. New York: Oxford University Press 1977.

Harms, William F. "Adaptation and Moral Realism." *Biology and Philosophy* 15 (2000): 699–712.

Harpur, Timothy J., A. Ralph Hakstian, and Robert D. Hare. "Factor Structure of the Psychopathy Checklist." *Journal of Consulting and Clinical Psychology* 56 (1988): 741–47.

Harpur, Timothy J., Stephen D. Hart, and Robert D. Hare. "The Personality of the Psychopath." In Paul T. Costa Jr. and Thomas A. Widiger, eds., *Personality Disorders and the Five Factor Model of Personality.* Washington, DC: American Psychological Association 1994, 149–73.

Harris, J.R. *The Nurture Assumption.* New York: Simon and Schuster 1998.

Hart, Stephen D., and Robert D. Hare. "Psychopathy: Assessment and Association with Criminal Conduct." In David M. Stoff, James Breiling, and Jack D. Maser, eds., *Handbook of Antisocial Behavior.* New York: John Wiley & Sons 1997, 22–35.

Heine, Berndt. "The Mountain People: Some Notes on the Ik of North-Eastern Uganda." *Africa* 55 (1984): 3–16.

Herman, Barbara. *The Practice of Moral Judgment.* London: Harvard University Press 1993.

Honore, Erika K., and Peter H. Klopfer. *A Concise Survey of Animal Behavior.* San Diego: Academic Press 1990.

Hudson, W.D. *A Century of Moral Philosophy.* New York: St Martin's Press 1980.

– *Ethical Intuitionism.* London: Macmillan 1967.

– *Modern Moral Philosophy.* London: Macmillan 1970.

– ed. *The Is-Ought Question.* London: Macmillan 1969.

Hughes, William. "Richard's Defense of Evolutionary Ethics." *Biology and Philosophy* 1 (1986): 305–15.

Humberstone, I. Lloyd. "Direction of Fit." *Mind* 101 (1992): 59–83.

Hume, David. *A Treatise of Human Nature.* Ed. David Fate Norton and Mary J. Norton. Oxford: Oxford University Press 2000.

Hunczak, Taras. "Ukrainian-Jewish Relations during the Soviet and Nazi Occupations." In Yury Boshyk, ed., *Ukraine during World War II: History and Its Aftermath.* Edmonton: Canadian Institute of Ukrainian Studies 1986, 39–57.

– "The Ukrainian Losses during World War II." In Michael Berenbaum, ed., *A Mosaic of Victims: Non-Jews Persecuted and Murdered by the Nazis.* New York: New York University Press 1990, 116–27.

Hurd, James P., ed. *Investigating the Biological Foundations of Human Morality.* Lewiston: The Edwin Mellen Press 1996.

Huxley, Thomas H. "Evolution and Ethics." Rpt. in Matthew H. Nitecki and Doris V. Nitecki, eds., *Evolutionary Ethics.* Albany, NY: State University of New York Press 1993, 29–80.

Jeffery, C.R., ed. *Biology and Crime.* Beverly Hills: Sage Publications 1979.

Jones, Ward E. "Explaining Our Beliefs: Non-Epistemic Believing and Doxastic Instability." *Philosophical Studies* 111 (2002): 217–49.

Joyce, R. "Darwinian Ethics and Error." *Biology and Philosophy* 15 (2000): 713–32.

Kagan, Shelly. *The Limits to Morality.* Oxford: Clarendon Press 1989.

– "The Structure of Normative Ethics." *Philosophical Perspectives* 6 (1992): 223–42.

Keeley, Lawrence H. *War before Civilization.* New York and London: Oxford University Press 1996.

Kekes, John. "Moral Intuition." *American Philosophical Quarterly* 23 (1986): 83–93.

Kitcher, Philip. "Psychological Altruism, Evolutionary Origins and Moral Rules." *Philosophical Studies* 89, nos. 2–3 (1998): 283–316.

Krawchenko, Bohdan. "Soviet Ukraine under Nazi Occupation, 1941–44." In Yury Boshyk, ed., *Ukraine during World War II: History and Its Aftermath.* Edmonton: Canadian Institute of Ukrainian Studies 1986, 15–37.

Leon, Mark. "Responsible Believers." *Monist* 85 (2002): 421–35.

Levenson, Michael R. "Rethinking Psychopathy." *Theory and Psychology* 2 (1992): 51–71.

Levi, Israel, and Sidney Morgenbesser. "Belief and Disposition." *American Philosophical Quarterly* 1 (1964): 221–32.

Lewis, David. "Dispositional Theories of Value." *Aristotelian Society, Supplementary Volume* 63 (1989): 113–37.

Lindzey, G., and E. Aronson, eds., *Handbook of Social Psychology.* 2d ed. Reading, MA: Addison-Wesley 1985.

Link, Nancy F., Shawn E. Scherer, and P. Niall Byrne. "Moral Judgment and Moral Conduct in the Psychopath." *Canadian Psychiatric Association Journal* 22 (1977): 341–6.

Locke, Don. "The Choice between Lives." *Philosophy* 57 (1982): 453–75.

– "The Trivializability of Universalizability." In Wilfrid Sellars and John Hospers, eds., *Readings in Ethical Theory.* Englewood Cliffs, NJ: Prentice-Hall 1970, 517–28.

Lycan, William G. "Why Should We Care Whether Our Beliefs Are True?" *Philosophy and Phenomenological Research* 51 (1991): 201–5.

Mackie, J.L. *Ethics: Inventing Right and Wrong.* Harmondsworth, England: Penguin 1977.

– "The Law of the Jungle: Moral Alternatives and Principles of Evolution." *Philosophy* 53 (1978): 455–64.

Matilal, Bimal Krishan. "Ethical Relativism and Confrontation of Cultures." In Michael Krausz, ed., *Relativism: Interpretation and Confrontation.* Notre Dame, IN: University of Notre Dame Press 1989, 339–62.

May, Larry, Marylin Friedman, and Andy Clark, eds., *Mind and Morals: Essays on Cognitive Science and Ethics*. Cambridge, MA: MIT Press 1996.

Mayr, Ernst. "How to Carry Out the Adaptationist Program?" In David R. Keller and Frank B. Golley, eds., *The Philosophy of Ecology: From Science to Synthesis*. Athens, GA, and London: The University of Georgia Press 2000, 277–87. Rpt. from *American Naturalist* 121 (1983): 324–33.

McCord, William, and Joan McCord. *The Psychopath: An Essay on the Criminal Mind*. Princeton, NJ: Van Nostrand 1964.

– *Psychopathy and Delinquency*. New York: Grune & Stratton 1956.

McMahan, Jeff. "Death and the Value of Life." *Ethics* 99 (1988): 32–61.

McNamee, Sharie. "Moral Behavior, Moral Development and Motivation." *Journal of Moral Education* 7 (1977): 27–31.

Meyers, Robert G. "Evolution as a Ground for Realism." In Nicholas Rescher, ed., *Evolution, Cognition and Realism: Studies in Evolutionary Epistemology*. Lanham, MD: University Press of America 1990, 111–18.

Miller, Richard W. *Moral Differences*. Princeton, NJ: Princeton University Press 1992.

– "Ways of Moral Learning." *The Philosophical Review* 94 (1985): 507–56.

Milo, Ronald D. *Immorality*. Princeton, NJ: Princeton University Press 1984.

Mitchell, Jim, and Richard A. Dodder. "Types of Neutralization and Types of Delinquency." *Journal of Youth and Adolescence* 12 (1983): 307–18.

Monroe, Kristen R., Michael C. Barton, and Ute Klingemann. "Altruism and the Theory of Rational Action: Rescuers of Jews in Nazi Europe." *Ethics* 101 (1990): 103–22.

Murphy, Jeffrie G. "Moral Death: A Kantian Essay on Psychopathy." *Ethics* 82 (1972): 284–98.

Nachshon, Israel. "Hemisphere Function in Violent Offenders." In Terrie E. Moffit and Sarnoff A. Mednick, eds., *Biological Contributions to Crime Causation*. Dordrecht: Martinus Nijhoff Publishers 1988, 55–67.

Nagel, Thomas. "Death." In his *Mortal Questions*. Cambridge: Cambridge University Press 1979, 1–10.

– "Ethics as an Autonomous Theoretical Subject." In Gunther S. Stent, ed., *Morality as a Biological Phenomenon*. Berlin: Dahlem Konferenzen 1978, 221–31.

– *The Possibility of Altruism*. Oxford: Clarendon Press 1970.

Nisbett, R., and L. Ross. *Human Inference: Strategies and Shortcomings of Social Judgment*. Englewood Cliffs, NJ: Prentice-Hall 1980.

Nozick, Robert. *Invariances: The Structure of the Objective World.* Cambridge, MA: The Belknap Press of Harvard University Press 2001.

O'Connor, D.J. "Beliefs, Dispositions, and Actions." *Proceedings of the Aristotelian Society* 69 (1969): 1–16.

Oliner, Samuel P. "Rescuers of Jews during the Holocaust." In Michael Berenbaum and Abraham J. Peck, eds., *The Holocaust and History: The Known, the Unknown, the Disputed, and the Reexamined.* Bloomington, IN: Indiana University Press 1998, 678–90.

Otsuka, Michael. "Killing the Innocent in Self-Defense." *Philosophy and Public Affairs* 23 (1994): 74–94.

Packer, Martin, Norma Haan, Paolo Theodorou, and Gary Yabrove. "Moral Action of Four-Year-Olds." In Norma Haan, Eliane Aerts, and Bruce A.B. Cooper. *On Moral Grounds: The Search for Practical Morality.* New York: New York University Press 1985, 276–305.

Patrick, Christopher J., and Bruce N. Cuthbert. "Emotion in the Criminal Psychopath." *Journal of Abnormal Psychology* 103 (1994): 523–34.

Pennock, Robert T. "Moral Darwinism: Ethical Evidence for the Descent of Man." *Biology and Philosophy* 10 (1995): 287–307.

Pincoffs, Edmund L. *Quandaries and Virtues: Against Reductivism in Ethics.* Laurence, KS: University of Kansas Press 1986.

Price, H.H. *Belief.* London: George Allen & Unwin 1969.

Quirk, Randolph, Sidney Greenbaum, Geoffrey Leach, and Jan Svartvik. *A Comprehensive Grammar of the English Language.* London: Longman 1985.

Rachels, James. *Created from Animals: The Moral Implications of Darwinism.* Oxford: Oxford University Press 1990.

Raine, Adrian. "Evoked Potentials and Antisocial Behavior." In Terrie E. Moffit and Sarnoff A. Mednick, eds., *Biological Contributions to Crime Causation.* Dordrecht: Martinus Nijhoff Publishers 1988, 14–39.

Raphael, D.D., ed. *British Moralists.* 2 vols. Oxford: Clarendon Press 1969.

Redfield, Robert. *The Primitive World and Its Transformation.* Ithaca, NY: Cornell University Press 1953.

Rescher, Nicholas. *A Useful Inheritance: Evolutionary Aspects of the Theory of Knowledge.* Lanham, MD: Rowman and Littlefield 1990.

Richards, Robert J. "Birth, Death, and Resurrection of Evolutionary Ethics." In Matthew H. Nitecki and Doris V. Nitecki, eds., *Evolutionary Ethics.* Albany, NY: State University of New York Press 1993, 113–32.

– "Darwin's Romantic Biology: The Foundations of His Evolutionary Ethics." In Jane Maienschein and Michael Ruse, eds., *Biology and the Foundations of Ethics.* Cambridge: Cambridge University Press 1999, 113–53.

– "A Defense of Evolutionary Ethics." *Biology and Philosophy* 1 (1986): 265–93.

– "Dutch Objections to Evolutionary Ethics." *Biology and Philosophy* 4 (1989): 331–43.

– "Justification through Biological Faith: A Rejoinder." *Biology and Philosophy* 1 (1989): 337–54.

Richerson, Peter J., and Robert Boyd. *Not by Genes Alone: How Culture Transformed Human Evolution*. Chicago and London: The University of Chicago Press 2005.

Rieber, R.W., and Harold Vetter. "The Language of the Psychopath." *Journal of Psycholinguistic Research* 23 (1994): 1–28.

Riedl, Rupert. *Biology of Knowledge: The Evolutionary Basis of Reason*. Chichester, England: John Wiley & Sons 1984.

Rigterink, Roger J. "What Are Beliefs (If They Are Anything at All)?" *Metaphilosophy* 22 (1991): 101–14.

Robins, Lee N., Jayson Tipp, and Thomas Przybeck. "Antisocial Personality." In Lee N. Robins and Darrel A. Regier, eds., *Psychiatric Disorders in America: The Epidemiological Catchment Area Study*. New York: The Free Press 1991, 258–90.

Rogers, A.R. "Does Biology Constrain Culture?" *American Anthropologist* 90 (1988): 819–31.

Rosenberg, Alexander. "The Biological Justification of Ethics: A Best-Case Scenario." In Paul Thompson, ed., *Issues in Evolutionary Ethics*. Albany, NY: State University of New York Press 1995, 351–74. Rpt. from *Social Philosophy and Policy* 8 (1989): 86–101.

Ross, W.D. *The Right and the Good*. Oxford: Clarendon Press 1930.

Rottschaefer, William A. *The Biology and Psychology of Moral Agency*. New York: Cambridge University Press 1998.

– "Evolutionary Ethics: An Irresistible Temptation." *Philosophy and Biology* 12 (1997): 369–84.

– "Evolutionary Naturalistic Justifications of Morality." *Philosophy and Biology* 6 (1991): 341–9.

– "Naturalizing Ethics: The Biology and Psychology of Moral Agency." *Zygon* 35 (2000): 253–86.

Rottschaefer, William A., and David Martinsen. "The Insufficience of Supervenient Explanations of Moral Actions: Really Taking Darwin and the Naturalistic Fallacy Seriously." *Philosophy and Biology* 6 (1991): 439–5.

– "Really Taking Darwin Seriously: An Alternative to Michael Ruse's Darwinian Ethics." In Paul Thompson, ed., *Issues in Evolutionary Ethics*.

Albany, NY: State University of New York Press 1995, 375–408. Rpt. from *Biology and Philosophy* 5 (1990): 149–73.

Rowe, David C. "Inherited Dispositions toward Learning Delinquent and Criminal Behavior: New Evidence." In Lee Ellis and Harry Hoffman, eds., *Crime in Biological, Social and Moral Contexts*. New York: Praeger 1990, 121–33.

Ruse, Michael. *The Darwinian Paradigm*. London: Routledge 1989.

– "Evolutionary Ethics: A Defence." In Holmes Rolston III, ed. *Biology, Ethics and the Origin of Life*. Boston: Jones and Bartlett 1995, 93–112.

– "Is Rape Wrong on Andromeda?" In Edward Regis Jr, ed., *Extraterrestrials: Science and Alien Intelligence*. Cambridge: Cambridge University Press 1985, 43–78.

– "The New Evolutionary Ethics." In Matthew H. Nitecki and Doris V. Nitecki, eds., *Evolutionary Ethics*. Albany, NY: State University of New York Press 1993, 133–62.

– *Philosophy of Biology Today*. Albany, NY: State University of New York Press 1988.

– "The Significance of Evolution." In Peter Singer, ed., *A Companion to Ethics*. Oxford: Basil Blackwell 1991, 500–10.

– *Taking Darwin Seriously*. Oxford: Blackwell 1986.

Ruse, Michael, and Edward O. Wilson. "The Evolution of Ethics." In Michael Ruse, ed., *Philosophy of Biology*. New York: Macmillan 1989, 313–17.

– "Moral Philosophy as Applied Science." *Philosophy* 61 (1986): 173–92.

Ryan, C. "Self-Defense, Pacifism, and the Possibility of Killing." *Ethics* 93 (1983): 508–24.

Ryan, James A. "Taking the 'Error' out of Ruse's Error Theory." *Biology and Philosophy* 12 (1997): 385–97.

Sarason, Irwin G., and Barbara R. Sarason. *Abnormal Psychology: The Problem of Maladaptive Behavior*. 7th ed. Englewood Cliffs, NJ: Prentice-Hall 1993.

Sayre-McCord, Geoffrey. "Introduction: The Many Moral Realisms." In his *Essays on Moral Realism*. Ithaca, NY: Cornell University Press 1988, 1–23.

– "Moral and Explanatory Importance." In his *Essays on Moral Realism*. Ithaca, NY: Cornell University Press 1988, 256–81.

Schachter, Daniel L. *The Seven Sins of Memory*. Boston: Houghton Mifflin Company 2001.

Schechtman, Marya. "The Truth about Memory." *Philosophical Psychology* 7 (1994): 3–18.

Schulsinger, F. "Psychopathy: Heredity and Environment." *International Journal of Mental Health* 1 (1972): 190–206.

Sesardic, Neven. "Altruism." *British Journal for the Philosophy of Science* 50 (1999): 457–66.

– "Recent Work on Human Altruism and Evolution." *Ethics* 106 (1995): 128–57.

Shaw, William H. "How to Do Ethics: A Question of Method." *Metaphilosophy* 13 (1982): 117–30.

– "Intuition and Moral Philosophy." *American Philosophical Quarterly* 17 (1980): 127–34.

Shweder, Richard A., Manamohan Mahapatra, and Joan G. Miller. "Culture and Development." In Jerome Kagan and Sharon Lamb, eds., *The Emergence of Morality in Young Children*. Chicago: University of Chicago Press 1987, 1–82.

Simpson, George G. "The Biological Nature of Man." *Science* 152 (1966): 472–8.

– "Naturalistic Ethics and the Social Sciences." *American Psychologist* 21 (1966): 27–36.

Singer, Peter. *The Expanding Circle: Ethics and Sociobiology*. New York: Farrar, Straus & Giroux 1981.

– "Utility and the Survival Lottery." *Philosophy* 52 (1977): 218–22.

Slote, Michael. *Common-Sense Morality and Consequentialism*. London: Routledge & Kegan Paul 1985.

Smart, B.J. "Understanding and Justifying Self-Defense." *International Journal of Moral and Social Studies* 4 (1989): 231–44.

Smetana, Judith G. "Preschool Children's Conception of Moral and Social Rules." *Child Development* 56 (1981): 1333–6.

Smith, Michael. "Dispositional Theories of Value." *The Aristotelian Society, Supplementary Volume* 63 (1989): 89–111.

– "The Humean Theory of Motivation." *Mind* 96 (1987): 36–61.

– *The Moral Problem*. Oxford: Blackwell 1994.

Smith, Robert J. *The Psychopath in Society*. New York: Academic Press 1978.

Sober, Elliott. "Disentangling the Phenotypes." In Matthew H. Nitecki and Doris V. Nitecki, eds., *Evolutionary Ethics*. Albany, NY: State University of New York Press 1993, 199–216.

– *The Nature of Selection: Evolutionary Theory in Philosophical Focus*. Cambridge, MA: MIT Press 1984.

– *Philosophy of Biology*. Boulder and San Francisco: Westview 1993.

– "Prospects for an Evolutionary Ethics." In his *From a Biological Point of View*. New York: Cambridge University Press 1994, 93–113.

– "When Natural Selection and Culture Conflict." In Holmes Rolston III, ed., *Biology, Ethics and the Origin of Life*. Boston: Jones and Bartlett 1995, 141–61.

Sober, Elliott, and David Sloan Wilson. *Unto Others: The Evolution and Psychology of Unselfish Behavior.* Cambridge, MA: Harvard University Press 1998.

Stephenson, Geoffrey M. *The Psychology of Criminal Justice*. Oxford: Blackwell 1992.

Sterelny, Kim, and Paul E. Griffiths. *Sex and Death: An Introduction to Philosophy of Biology.* Chicago: University of Chicago Press 1999.

Stingl, Michael. "All the Monkeys Aren't in the Zoo: Evolutionary Ethics and the Possibility of Moral Knowledge." In Richmond Campbell and Bruce Hunter, eds., *Moral Epistemology Naturalized*. Calgary: University of Calgary Press 2000, 245–65.

Stout, Martha. *The Sociopath Next Door.* New York: Broadway Books 2005.

Swanson, M.C.J., R.C. Bland, and S.C. Newman. "Antisocial Personality Disorders." *Acta Psychiatrica Scandinavica* Supplement 376 (1994): 63–70.

Sykes, G.M., and D. Matza. "Techniques of Neutralization: A Theory of Delinquency." *American Sociological Review* 22 (1957): 664–79.

Taurek, John M. "Should the Numbers Count?" *Philosophy and Public Affairs* 6 (1977): 293–316.

Tec, Nechama. "Reflections on Rescuers." In Michael Berenbaum and Abraham J. Peck, eds., *The Holocaust and History: The Known, the Unknown, the Disputed, and the Reexamined*. Bloomington, IN: Indiana University Press 1998, 651–62.

– *When Light Pierced the Darkness: Christian Rescue of Jews in Nazi-Occupied Poland*. New York and London: Oxford University Press 1986.

Thomas, Laurence. "Biological Moralism." *Biology and Philosophy* 1 (1986): 316–25.

Thompson, Paul. "Evolutionary Ethics: Its Origin and Contemporary Face." *Zygon* 34 (1999): 473–84.

Thomson, Judith Jarvis. "A Defense of Abortion." *Philosophy and Public Affairs* 1 (1971): 47–66.

– "Self-Defense." *Philosophy and Public Affairs* 20 (1991): 283–310.

Thurman, Quint. "Deviance and the Neutralization of Moral Commitment: An Empirical Analysis." *Deviant Behavior* 5 (1984): 291–304.

Tooley, Michael. "Abortion and Infanticide." *Philosophy and Public Affairs* 2 (1972): 37–65.

Trammell, R. "Taking Life and Saving Life." *Journal of Philosophy* 72 (1975): 131–7.

Trigg, Roger. "Evolutionary Ethics." *Biology and Philosophy* 1 (1986): 325–35.

Trivers, R.L. "The Evolution of Reciprocal Altruism." *The Quarterly Review of Biology* 46 (1971): 35–57.

– *Social Evolution*. Menlo Park: Benjamin/Cummings 1985.

Turiel, Elliott. *The Development of Social Knowledge: Morality and Convention*. Cambridge: Cambridge University Press 1983.

Turiel, Elliott, Melanie Killen, and Charles C. Helwig. "Morality: Its Structure, Functions and Vagaries." In Jerome Kagan and Sharon Lamb, eds., *The Emergence of Morality in Young Children*. Chicago: University of Chicago Press 1987, 155–243.

Turnbull, Colin M. *The Mountain People*. New York: Simon and Schuster 1972.

Urbanek, Adam. "Evolutionary Origin of Moral Principles." In Matthew H. Nitecki and Doris V. Nitecki, eds., *Evolutionary Ethics*. Albany, NY: State University of New York Press 1993, 325–36.

van den Berghe, Pierre L. *Human Family Systems: An Evolutionary View*. New York: Elsevier 1979.

van der Steen, Wim J. "Evolution and Altruism." *Journal of Value Inquiry* 33 (1999): 11–29.

Velleman, J. David. "On the Aim of Belief." In his *The Possibility of Practical Reason*. Oxford: Clarendon Press 2000, 244–81.

Viding, Essi, James R. Blair, Terrie E. Moffit, and Robert Plomin. "Evidence for Substantial Genetic Risk for Psychopathy in Seven-Year-Olds." *Journal of Child Psychology and Psychiatry* 46 (2005): 592–7.

Wade, Michael. "A Critical Review of the Models of Group Selection." *The Quarterly Review of Biology* 53 (1978): 101–14.

Walker, Stephen. *Animal Thought*. London: Routledge & Kegan Paul 1983.

Wallace, R. Jay. "How to Argue about Practical Reason." *Mind* 99 (1990): 355–85.

Waller, Bruce N. "Moral Commitment without Objectivity or Illusion: Comments on Ruse and Woolcock." *Biology and Philosophy* 11 (1996): 245–54.

– *The Natural Selection of Autonomy*. Alban, NY: State University of New York Press 1998.

– "What Rationality Adds to Animal Rationality." *Biology and Philosophy* 12 (1997): 341–56.

Wasserman, David. "Justifying Self-Defense." *Philosophy and Public Affairs* 16 (1987): 356–78.

Weiss, Aharon. "The Holocaust and Ukrainian Victims." In Michael Berenbaum, ed., *A Mosaic of Victims: Non-Jews Persecuted and Murdered by the Nazis*. New York: New York University Press 1990, 109–15.

Wesson, Robert. *Beyond Natural Selection*. Cambridge, MA: MIT Press 1991.

Weston, Donna R., and Elliott Turiel. "Act-Rule Relations: Children's Concepts of Social Rules." *Developmental Psychology* 16 (1980): 417–24.

Williams, Bernard. "Deciding to Believe." In his *Problems of the Self: Philosophical Papers* 1956–1972. Cambridge: Cambridge University Press 1973, 136–51.

– "Ethical Consistency." In Geoffrey Sayre-McCord, ed., *Essays on Moral Realism*. Ithaca, NY: Cornell University Press 1988, 41–58.

– *Ethics and the Limits of Philosophy*. Cambridge, MA: Harvard University Press 1985.

– "Evolutionary Theory: Epistemology and Ethics." In Alan Grafen, ed., *Evolution and Its Influence*. Oxford: Clarendon Press 1989, 93–106.

Williams, George C. *Adaptation and Natural Selection*. Princeton: Princeton University Press 1966.

– "Huxley's Evolution and Ethics in Sociobiological Perspective." In Paul Thompson, ed., *Issues in Evolutionary Ethics*. Albany, NY: State University of New York Press 1995, 317–49.

– "Mother Nature Is a Wicked Old Witch." In Matthew H. Nitecki and Doris V. Nitecki, eds., *Evolutionary Ethics*. Albany, NY: State University of New York Press 1993, 217–32.

– *Natural Selections: Domains Levels, and Challenges*. New York: Cambridge University Press 1992.

– *The Pony Fish's Glow*. New York: Basic Books 1997.

– "A Sociobiological Expansion of *Evolution and Ethics*." In James Paradis and George C. Williams, eds., *Evolution & Ethics*. Princeton, NJ: Princeton University Press 1989, 179–214.

Williams, Patricia A. "Can Beings Whose Ethics Evolved Be Ethical Beings?" In Matthew H. Nitecki and Doris V. Nitecki, eds., *Evolutionary Ethics*. Albany, NY: State University of New York Press 1993, 233–40.

– "Evolved Ethics Re-examined: The Theory of Robert J. Richards." *Biology and Philosophy* 5 (1990): 451–7.

Williamson, S., T.J. Harpur, and R.D. Hare. "Abnormal Processing of Affective Words by Psychopaths." *Psychophysiology* 28 (1991): 260–73.

Wilson, E.O. *Sociobiology: The New Synthesis*. Cambridge, MA: Harvard University Press 1975.

Woodsworth, M., and S. Porter. "In Cold Blood: Characteristics of Criminal Homicide as a Function of Psychopathy." *Journal of Abnormal Psychology* 111 (2002): 436–45.

Woolcock, Peter G. "The Case against Evolutionary Ethics Today." In Jane Maienschein and Michael Ruse, eds., *Biology and the Foundations of Ethics*. Cambridge: Cambridge University Press 1999, 276–306.

– "Ruse's Darwinian Meta-Ethics: A Critique." *Biology and Philosophy* 8 (1993): 423–39.

Wuketits, Franz M. "Darwinism: Still a Challenge to Philosophy." *Zygon* 23 (1988): 455–67.

Yanal, Robert J. "The Unimportance of Being Worthless." *American Philosophical Quarterly* 23 (1986): 95–103.

Index